# THE UNEXPLAINED

# LOST WORLDS
## AND FORGOTTEN SECRETS

Produced by Carlton Books Limited
20 Mortimer Street
London, W1N 7RD

Text and Design copyright © Carlton Books Limited 2001

First published in hardback edition in 2001 by Chelsea House Publishers, a subsidiary of
Haights Cross Communications. Printed and bound in Dubai.

First Printing
1 3 5 7 9 8 6 4 2

The Chelsea House World Wide Web address is http://www.chelseahouse.com

Library of Congress Cataloging-in-Publication Data applied for

Historic Realms of Marvels and Miracles  ISBN:  0-7910-6076-4
Ancient Worlds, Ancient Mysteries  ISBN:  0-7910-6077-2
Lost Worlds and Forgotten Secrets  ISBN:  0-7910-6078-0
We Are Not Alone  ISBN:  0-7910-6079-9
Imagining Other Worlds  ISBN:  0-7910-6080-2
Coming from the Skies  ISBN:  0-7910-6081-0
Making Contact  ISBN:  0-7910-6082-9

# THE UNEXPLAINED

# LOST WORLDS
## AND FORGOTTEN SECRETS

### Riddles of Earth and Beyond

Dr Karl P.N. Shuker

Chelsea House Publishers

Philadelphia

# THE
# UNEXPLAINED
# LOST WORLDS
## AND FORGOTTEN SECRETS

Historic Realms of Marvels and Miracles

Ancient Worlds, Ancient Mysteries

We Are Not Alone

Imagining Other Worlds

Coming From the Skies

Making Contact

# CONTENTS

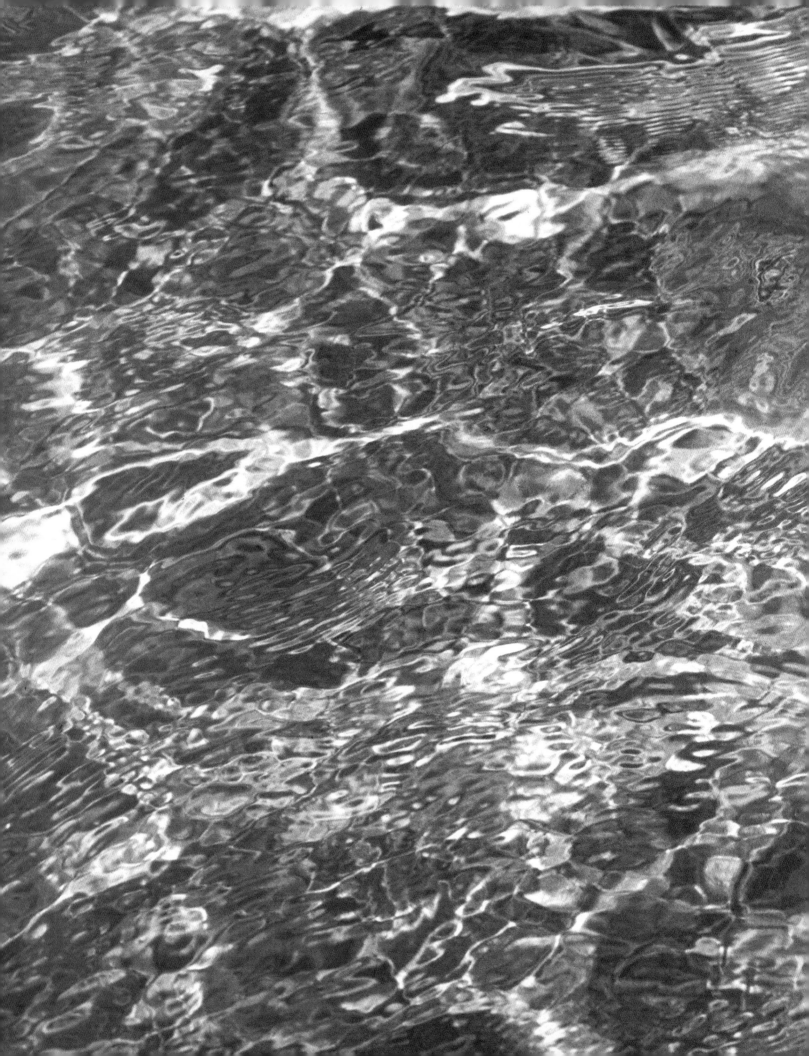

# Continents, Coincidences and Curiosities

## ATLANTIS

In his books *Timaeus* and *Critias*, the famous philosopher Plato (c.428–c.348 BC) wrote of a vast island continent called Atlantis. Believed to be situated to the west of the Pillars of Hercules (the Straits of Gibraltar) and originally inhabited by a highly advanced civilization, it had been destroyed over nine thousand years earlier by violent earthquakes and floods. This had occurred within the space of a single day and night, and the continent had sunk beneath the depths of the seas. According to Plato, his sources for this account were the works of an Athenian scholar called Solon, who had learnt of it when he visited priests and archives (now lost) in Egypt in c.600 BC.

Since then, numerous theories have been aired regarding the erstwhile locality of Atlantis. Suggestions have included such far-flung, varyingly feasible sites as Greenland, Spitzbergen, Malta, the Azores, Anatolia, Mongolia, Sweden, Heligoland, Nigeria, Mexico, Brazil and South Africa.

Naturally, one might expect that the most reasonable site for Atlantis would be in the mid-Atlantic. Yet there has been no geological upheaval consistent with the sinking of a continental land mass here for at least several million years.

In academic circles, one of the most popular theories is that Plato's account was inspired by the relatively abrupt collapse of Crete's once-mighty Minoan empire and that this had been caused by the cataclysmic volcanic explosion of the Aegean island of Thera, whose modern-day remnant is Santorini. Yet researchers concede that there are many

*Plato's account of Atlantis was based on ancient Egyptian sources.*

notable discrepancies between Crete's history and Plato's account of Atlantis – not least of which is that Atlantis supposedly vanished nine thousand years before Solon's time, whereas Thera was destroyed a mere nine hundred years before. In any case, there is no certainty that Thera's eruption and the Minoan civilization's collapse

was a direct cause-and-effect situation.

In 1968, however, a dramatically new Atlantean locality was revealed – and not in the Mediterranean, but within the Atlantic Ocean itself. The location was the Bahamas, where a local diver called Bonefish Sam showed Dr J. Manson Valentine – a Miami zoologist who was also a keen amateur archaeologist – an underwater anomaly well known to local tourist guides and fishermen but seemingly unknown to scientists. Nowadays known as the Bimini Road (though more similar to a low wall), it was situated in shallow water at Paradise Point, about a kilometre (half a mile) to the west of North Bimini Island, and in the words of Valentine, it comprised:

*... an extensive pavement of rectangular and polygonal flat stones of varying size and thickness, obviously shaped and accurately aligned to form a convincing artifactual pattern ... Some were absolutely rectangular and some approaching perfect squares.*

The longest row of these stones (each stone weighing between one and ten tonnes) ran for nearly 500 metres (1600 feet) and ended in a 90 degree bend. Nevertheless, not everyone shared Valentine's belief that the Bimini Road was of human construction. In 1970, archaeologist Professor John Hall from Miami University pointed out that

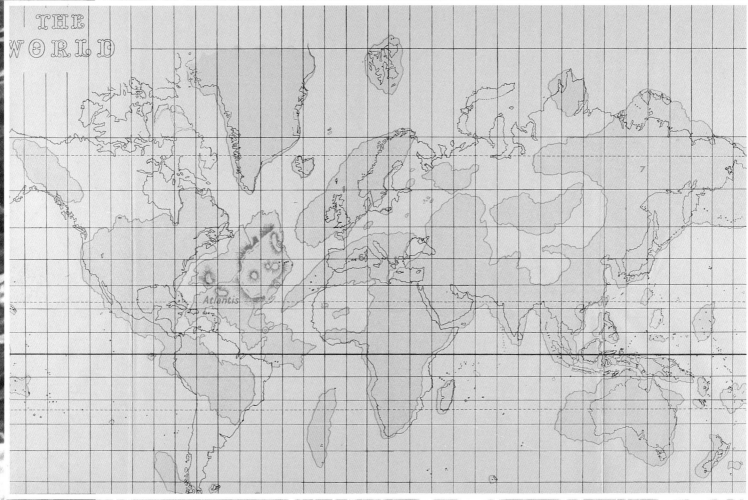

*The "lost continents" of Atlantis and Lemuria particularly interested the Theosophical Society, which published this map in W. Scott Elliott's* **The Story of Atlantis and the Lost Lemuria** *(1896).*

layers of rock with regular block-like fractures like the Bimini examples can be formed by natural means and constitute a well-documented phenomenon known as Pleistocene beach-rock erosion and cracking.

However, the Bimini Road was not the only unexpected discovery made in this area of the Bahamian sea-bed. In 1975, Dr David D. Zink, author of *The Stones of Atlantis*, discovered a stone building block containing an unequivocally man-made tongue-and-groove joint. And several fluted marble columns have been found here by Count Pino Turolla (yet marble is not native to the Bahamas). Sceptics of the Atlantis theory have dismissed these discoveries as ballast from historically recent shipwrecks (noting the presence nearby of a modern-day packing crate).

Even so, there is still no conclusive evidence that ballast formed from items such as these has ever been utilized. As for the Bimini Road, there is a theory

that can combine both of the opposing views. What if this structure is indeed of natural origin, but was purposefully used by a vanished race of people? In 1970, Dr R. Cedric Leonard explored some enigmatic temple-like ruins sighted off Andros Island, near Bimini. Investigations of Bimini's underwater mysteries are still continuing: one day their true story may finally be known.

Perhaps the most intriguing correlation between this site and Atlantis derives from the many Atlantis-related predictions made by the famous American psychic Edgar Cayce, for these include the following prophecy:

*A portion of the temples [of Atlantis] may yet be discovered under the slime of ages of sea water near Bimini ... Expect it in '68 and '69; not so far away!*

Cayce died in 1945, more than 20 years before the discovery of the Bimini Road – in 1968.

# JAMES DEAN – RIDDLES OF A REBEL'S DEATH

It was a September evening in 1955, and Alec Guinness, destined to become one of Britain's greatest stars of stage and screen, had arrived in Los Angeles to make his first Hollywood film, *The Swan*. While looking for a table at a restaurant, he and his companion, scriptwriter Thelma Moss, met a 24-year-old American actor in jeans and a sweatshirt who invited them to join him. First of all, however, he asked them to come and see something, which proved to be a shining, silver-coloured racing car, a Porsche 550 Spyder, that he had just bought and was his pride and joy. It was certainly very eyecatching, but for

*James Dean (left) with Rock Hudson and Elizabeth Taylor at a 1955 Hollywood press lunch to publicize* **Giant**, *the film he completed just days before his death. Inset: Jimmy's car, a Porsche 550 Spyder, which he nicknamed "Little Bastard".*

some inexplicable reason Guinness felt uneasy. As he recalled many years later in his autobiography *Blessings in Disguise*, he couldn't shake off the feeling that there was something sinister about it.

Suddenly, almost as if he were someone else, merely listening to the words, rather than being the person actually uttering them, Guinness found himself earnestly asking this young fair-haired actor never to get into the car. As he spoke, Guinness looked at his watch, and then said: "It is now ten o'clock, Friday the 23rd of September, 1955. If you get in that car you will be found dead in it by this time next week."

A little startled, the youth laughed, and Guinness apologized for his strange outburst. Seven days later, however,

shortly before six o'clock on the evening of 30 September, his unnerving prediction was fulfilled: during the hours that followed, Guinness and the whole world would be stunned to learn of the young actor's untimely death, killed instantly in a collision with a black Ford limousine near the tiny Californian town of Cholame while driving his new silver car to a race at Salinas.

The actor's name? James Dean.

Guinness was not alone in feeling uneasy about Jimmy's car. A few days before Jimmy set off in it, on what would prove to be his final drive, Ursula Andress, a former girlfriend, pleaded with him to change his mind: "I feel something about it. Don't go!" Jimmy asked her to accompany him, but she refused. That was the last time she saw him alive.

These are just two of many eerie coincidences linked with the tragic death of one of the most charismatic actors of all time, who seemed destined to become one of the greatest actors too, until he lost his life while driving what proved to be a singularly ill-fated car. For Jimmy was only the first of many to experience what has been dubbed "the curse" of his Porsche Spyder, which more than lived up to Jimmy's own name for it, "Little Bastard".

After Jimmy's death, car customizer George Barris purchased the crushed wreck of "Little Bastard" to salvage any parts that had not been damaged in the crash. As it was being unloaded in his garage, however, it somehow fell off its platform and hit one of his mechanics, breaking the man's leg. Shortly

*Wreckage from the accident in which Jimmy was killed; "Little Bastard" survived in various forms, causing further catastrophes.*

afterwards, a sports car driver bought two of its tyres and fitted them to his own vehicle: while he was driving it, both tyres inexplicably burst, the car skidded off the road and its driver was almost killed.

In October 1956, "Little Bastard" was directly involved in three separate accidents that took place in a single race at Pomona, California. The car being driven by one of the competitors, a surgeon called Dr William Eschrich, had recently been fitted with the engine from "Little Bastard". During that race, Eschrich barely escaped serious injury when his car overturned on a bend. Standing nearby at the time was policeman Bob Miller, who was hit in the face by one of Eschrich's wheels when it flew off in the accident. Tragically, physician Dr Troy McHenry was not so lucky as Eschrich and Miller. The back swinging arms holding his car's rear-end were from "Little Bastard", and during this same race he was killed instantly when his car unexpectedly went out of control and smashed into a tree.

Several months later, lorry driver George Barkuis was transporting "Little Bastard" when his truck ran off the road. Nevertheless, he was saved from

certain death by being thrown clear – only to be killed when this deadly car fell on top of him. And in a further incident, "Little Bastard" was one of many cars contained inside a garage that mysteriously caught fire. All of the cars were gutted, except for "Little Bastard", which was virtually unscathed.

In 1960, while travelling back to Barris by train from a show in Miami, "Little Bastard" vanished, apparently stolen. Thus the chain of catastrophes associated with this jinxed car was finally at an end – or was it? After all, what happened to the thief who stole "Little Bastard"? Did he live long enough to enjoy his ill-gotten (and ill-starred) prize, I wonder?

In the years since James Dean's death, countless unsubstantiated stories of a supernatural, sensationalistic nature have circulated. These include claims that people have been contacted by Jimmy from beyond the grave, that he was not really killed but was severely disfigured and was smuggled away to a secret clinic, and even that his ghost has been seen driving a spectral "Little Bastard" along that ill-fated stretch of road near Cholame in a recurring repetition of his fatal crash, ending with

the sounds of the collision. Make of such tales what you will.

What *is* fully substantiated is that Jimmy was well known for his quirky sense of humour, often wilfully dark, to shock and startle. When photographer Dennis Stock accompanied him in February 1955 on a visit to Fairmount, Indiana, where he had spent much of his youth, Jimmy decided to pose for some photos lying in an open coffin at Hunt's Funeral Parlour. In a picture taken by Sanford Roth, another photographer friend, he placed his head in a noose, and hung limply from it, as if his neck were broken. Presumably it is just an unpleasant coincidence that Jimmy's next (and final) return to Fairmount would also feature him inside a coffin at Hunt's Funeral Parlour, but this time as a corpse – with a broken neck.

Jimmy's razor-sharp, laconic wit, coupled with his passion for contemplation and analysis, have yielded a fund of memorable quotes, but for poignant accuracy few can match the line ad-libbed by him during an interview for a road safety television commercial, filmed less than a fortnight before his death. At the end of the commercial, the interviewer asked him for any advice to offer the viewers. Modifying his scripted reply, Jimmy quipped: "Take it easy driving. The life you might save might be *mine!*" Who could have believed that one of his last screen lines would be so chillingly prophetic?

*Giant* was Jimmy's last film, and was responsible for a very grotesque aspect of his death. Many people were shocked to learn that when his body was removed from his car's crumpled wreck after the collision, his face resembled that of an elderly man. However, Jimmy's final scenes in *Giant* had been as Jett Rink when old and dissipated, and as part of the make-up artists' procedure to achieve this illusion the hair on his forehead had been shaved off, giving him a receding hairline that aged him considerably. Just seven days after completing his work on *Giant*, Jimmy had set off to the race at Salinas. His hair hadn't had time to grow back, and so an ironic paradox was created in which a young actor whose untimely death ensured that he would remain forever youthful had died in the guise of an old man.

Jimmy once said: "I have a hunch that there are some things in life we just can't avoid. They'll happen to us, probably because we're built that way – we simply attract our own fate, make our own destiny." In life, one of Jimmy's greatest passions was bull-fighting – he even possessed the blood-stained cape of a real matador – but it would find expression in his death too, through a truly bizarre, savage coincidence. For according to John Howlett's book *James Dean: A Biography*, in the fatal crash Jimmy's body had been impaled, "torn open on the steering wheel, like a bullfighter on the horns".

✵

# THE MOVING STONES OF DEATH VALLEY

In a locality with a name like Death Valley, it is singularly ironic (or perversely apt, maybe) that what is normally inanimate elsewhere is

*The moving stones of Death Valley: a Californian rock legend.*

notoriously animate here.

Death Valley is one of California's most familiar national monuments, due in no small way to the scattering of stones on a dried-up lake in this valley known as the Racetrack playa; for these are the famous moving stones, which travel considerable distances across the Racetrack's hardened surface, seemingly of their own volition. Just as the stones themselves vary greatly in size, from pebbles to half-tonne boulders, their furrowed tracks differ very appreciably in form and length, and include zigzags, straight lines, gentle curves and distances ranging from a few metres to many hundreds.

For many years, the valley's roaming rocks bewildered the scientific world. In 1968, however, geologists Dr Robert Sharp and Dr Dwight Carey from the California Institute of Technology embarked upon a seven-year study of

this phenomenon, at the end of which they concluded that it could be satisfactorily explained by the occurrence of a specific set of ground and weather conditions – namely, the presence of strong winds following sufficient rainfall to cause a slippery surface on the Racetrack. As Dr Carey subsequently explained:

*The wind is able to pick up the rock and start it moving. It pushes aside the very slippery mud and slides along on the firm surface. It's probably moving a couple of feet per second as it rides off across the playa, and after a hundred, two hundred feet of movement, or sometimes just a very little movement, the stone will eventually come to rest as the wind dies down. I believe it's basically changes in the wind during the time when the rock is moving that cause the stone trails to be so variable.*

Until very recently, this mechanism was widely accepted as the explanation for the curious mobility of Death Valley's stones and rocks. In 1995, however, geologist John Reid from Hampshire College in Amherst, Massachusetts, offered a conflicting, alternative solution. He revealed that four years earlier, he had taken a party of students to the valley at a time when the set of conditions proposed by Sharp and Carey as the impetus for rock movement was prevalent there. Yet although Reid and his students were slipping across the Racetrack's surface with alarming ease, the rocks remained stubbornly immobile. Despite all their efforts, none of the members of the party was able to set any of the rocks in motion either.

Accordingly, Reid has suggested that the rocks will indeed move when blown by a strong wind, but only if they are frozen into an ice sheet, the ice's low coefficient of friction countering the resistance to movement created by the rocks' jagged, weathered surfaces. From moving stones to skating rocks? Only when someone is able to devise a means of directly recording their movements is science ever likely to know for sure.

✴

## BALL LIGHTNING AND SPOOKLIGHTS

It was summer 1958, and William Becker, now professor and industrial design researcher at Illinois University, was camping with five high-school friends in the upper Minnesota regions north of Grand Marias. One night during a heavy rainstorm, while sharing the back room of a deserted cabin with one friend, Becker was amazed to see a glowing ball of light quite literally squeeze through a small gap above the windowsill and float into their room. Slightly larger than a basketball, with a bright yellow-white perimeter but a darker orange core that contained writhing worm-like shapes, it slowly descended to the floor and glided silently over the rug. When it reached the wall, it shrank and vanished, but almost immediately a loud firecracker-like retort echoed from the other side of the wall.

During a thunderstorm one day in April 1915, a man was standing by a window in his home at Columbia, Missouri, when he heard a sound like a shotgun blast. Moments later, his telephone clicked and out of its mouthpiece emerged a small bubble-like sphere of light that floated towards him and then rolled around the windowsill before disappearing.

Marfa Mystery Lights

Over 100 years of unexplained flickering lights
Location: Mitchell Flats          Photo Date: 9/86
Photo Specifications: SLR w. 50mm lens at f1.8
Exposure: Less than 3 minutes   Film: EL 400
Researcher/Photographer:  ©1986  James Crocker

TEXAS

• Marfa

*The Marfa lights dart then hover in an animate display that defies imitation by earthbound or reflected light.*

On 25 August 1965, a basketball-sized ball of light, orange-red in colour, unexpectedly shot through the patio's fibreglass screen at the home of Clara Greenlee and her husband at Dunnellon, Florida. Aghast but armed, Clara whacked their fiery intruder with a fly-swatter and the luminous orb dropped to the floor, exploding with the sound of a rifle shot.

While watching television in an upstairs bedroom at her home in Rockville, Maryland, one February afternoon in 1989, Doris M. Humphrey suddenly noticed several small globes of white light, ranging in size from a marble to a ping-pong ball, hovering and dancing along the lengthy cord leading from the television to the wall outlet. They even swooped down into her wastepaper bin, inside which one loop of the cord had fallen, and then came out again and moved towards an artificial fireplace containing electric logs. Although the logs were not switched on, the tiny globes danced in the fireplace opening and then coalesced into a single sphere that bobbed up and down a few times before vanishing behind the logs.

These are just a few of the countless reports on file describing ball lightning – a mystifying phenomenon recorded throughout the world, yet particularly prevalent in North America. Ball lightning is exceedingly varied in form, but "typical" examples are spherical, can be any colour and range in size from marbles to basketballs. They frequently occur during thunderstorms, can materialize within an enclosed building, sometimes make a buzzing or hissing noise and leave behind a smell variously likened to sulphur or ozone. Their existence spans a few seconds to several minutes, and they generally float slowly but with a distinct "sense" of direction, rather than passively drifting. Some vanish silently, others with a loud explosion. They can cause great damage to inanimate objects, but rarely injure humans.

For many years, scientists dismissed ball lightning as an optical illusion – an after-image on the eye's retina resulting from a lightning flash. Such opinions were revised, however, when a dramatic case was witnessed by an extremely qualified eyewitness. On 19 March 1963,

Professor R.C. Jennison from the Electronic Laboratories at Kent University was aboard an Eastern Airlines flight from New York to Washington when an electrical storm enveloped the plane. Jennison reported that he saw a glowing ball of light with a diameter of just over 20 cm (8 inches) emerge from the pilot's cabin and float down the aisle, remaining about 75 cm (2½ feet) above the floor. It was also observed by an air hostess, who watched it disappear towards the toilet at the end of the aisle.

Many identities have been offered for ball lightning, including spheres of plasma, globes sustained by nuclear reaction, burning orbs of gas, forked lightning somehow compressed into a spherical form, and even tiny meteorites of antimatter. Today, Ohio scientists J.F. Corum and K.L. Corum are able to produce small balls of lightning in the laboratory, using a process involving high-voltage radio frequency. Japanese scientists too can create plasma globes, but there is still much to discover regarding this enigmatic phenomenon.

Very different from ball lightning are spooklights, which lack the former's potent, fiery power and more closely resemble will-o'-the-wisps (caused by marsh gas spontaneously igniting). North America has many famous examples, including the Marfa lights, frequently reported just east of this Texan town, in the direction of the Chinati mountains on the Mexican border. These resemble flickering yellow lanterns or headlights, about half as big as a basketball, darting rapidly through the air, sometimes hovering for a while and then vanishing. Although some reports may indeed be based upon unrecognized sightings of vehicle headlights, others have occurred in areas where there are no roads, and in many cases their animate displays effortlessly defy any imitation by earthbound or reflected headlights.

Even more eerie were the dancing balls of pulsating blue light that formerly frequented the graveyard at Silver Cliff, Colorado. In a detailed *New York Times* report for 20 August 1967, eyewitness W.T. Little revealed that several mundane explanations have been offered, including phosphorescence (caused by fungi) emitted by the graveyard's rotting

wooden tombstones and fences, glowing mineral ores in the ground (Silver Cliff is an old mining centre), and even the reflection of house lights from nearby homes. The last-mentioned theory, however, was disproved one night when every house switched off its lights and even the street lamps were extinguished, but the blue balls of light danced on regardless in the graveyard. In recent years, however, they have not been reported.

In contrast, the Brown Mountain lights of North Carolina are still eminently visible, variously described by eyewitnesses as "globular, glowing red, like toy fire-balloons", "a pale white light with a faint halo around it", or "not unlike a star from a bursting skyrocket". As noted by William R. Corliss in his invaluable *Handbook of Unusual Natural Phenomena*, they generally appear singly in succession, rising over the mountain's level ridge, then abruptly vanishing. Sometimes several appear together, and whereas their typical "lifetime" is less than a minute, they have been known to remain stationary above the ridge for up to 20 minutes. Once again, reflected headlights is a popular but unsatisfactory "official" solution.

It has been noted by many investigators, moreover, that the activity of some spooklights is almost intelligent, sometimes disconcertingly so – as in cases featuring balls of light that follow or entice people, then move out of their way when challenged. Could they be glowing swarms of insects? Or a more mysterious beast that lives high in the earth's atmosphere?

✪

# ABRAHAM LINCOLN, THE PARANORMAL PRESIDENT

The following words were spoken to his wife and some friends by a man describing to them an eerie, disturbing incident that had recently happened to him:

dream was murdered, on 14 April 1865. Afterwards, exactly as he had foreseen, his body did indeed lie in state in the East Room of the White House, and for a very good reason. The murdered dreamer was none other than Abraham Lincoln – the first President of the USA to be assassinated.

This is just one of many remarkable events with distinctly paranormal overtones that occurred during Lincoln's life – and even after his death too. For several visitors to the White House claim to have encountered his ghost there. Somewhat appropriately, the first such report appears to be from a First Lady – President Calvin Coolidge's wife, Grace, who said that she saw Lincoln looking out of a window in the Oval Office.

Another noteworthy sighting was by Queen Wilhelmina of the Netherlands, during a visit to President Franklin D. Roosevelt. One day, someone knocked on the door of her bedroom at the White House, and when she opened it she was amazed to see Abraham Lincoln standing outside in the hall, wearing his famous top hat and typical clothes dating from his own period of office. Roosevelt later informed her that the bedroom which she was occupying was referred to as the Lincoln Room and had been the scene of several previous sightings of the former president. One of Roosevelt's secretaries had even seen Lincoln sitting on the bed in this room, pulling on his boots. Several photographs purportedly depicting Lincoln's ghost have been publicized over the years too, but all of these have ultimately been exposed as fakes.

Even more macabre than Lincoln's prophetic dream of his own death are stories that a spectral version of the funeral train that took his body to Illinois for burial appears each year and follows this same route. According to a report in the *Albany Times*:

*Abraham Lincoln, photographic portrait c.1862.*

*About ten days ago I retired very late to bed and soon began to dream. There seemed to be a death-like stillness about me. Then I heard subdued sobs, as if a number of people were weeping. I thought I left my bed and wandered downstairs. There, the silence was broken by the same pitiful sobbing but the mourners were invisible. I went from room to room. No living person was in sight but the same mournful sounds of distress met me as I passed along. I was puzzled and alarmed.*

*Determined to find the cause of a state of things so mysterious and so shocking, I kept on until I arrived at the East Room. There I met with a sickening surprise. Before me was a catafalque on which rested a corpse wrapped in funeral vestments. Around it were stationed soldiers who were acting as guards and there was a throng of people, some gazing mournfully upon the corpse, whose face was covered, others weeping pitifully.*

*"Who is dead in the White House?" I demanded of one of the soldiers. "The President," was his answer. "He was killed by an assassin."*

Despite the disturbing nature of his words, no one paid a great deal of attention to them, until, just a few days later, the man who had dreamed this

*It passes noiselessly. If it is moonlight, clouds cover the moon as the phantom train goes by. After the pilot engine passes, the funeral train itself with flags and streamers rushes past. The track seems covered with black carpet and the coffin is seen in the center of the car, whilst all about it in the air and on the train behind are vast numbers of blue*

*President John F. Kennedy greets crowds in Dallas moments before his assassination on 22 November 1963. A bizarre set of coincidences surrounds the lives – and deaths – of Presidents Kennedy and Lincoln.*

*coated men, some with coffins on their backs, others leaning upon them.*

Just a legend? Perhaps. A fully confirmed fact, on the other hand, is that Lincoln's life was inexplicably connected by an uncanny array of coincidences – some trivial, others tragic – to that of another assassinated US President, John F. Kennedy.

When he was shot, President Kennedy was travelling in a Lincoln car, manufactured by Ford; President Lincoln was in the Ford Theatre when he was shot. Kennedy was advised not to go to Dallas by his secretary, who just happened to be called Evelyn Lincoln. Both presidents were shot in the back of the head, while travelling with their wives and after predicting their own deaths less than a day before. Kennedy had earlier told his wife that no one would be able to prevent it if someone wanted to kill him; Lincoln had earlier told one of his guards, W.H. Crook, that he was convinced there were people who wanted to kill him and that no one would succeed in stopping them. Morbid pessimism, or dire prophecy?

In any event, both were indeed assassinated: Kennedy by someone shooting from a warehouse who then ran into a theatre; Lincoln by someone shooting in a theatre who then ran into a storage barn. Both killers were themselves murdered too. A hundred years separated the election of the two future presidents to Congress (1846 and 1946 respectively) and also their election to the presidency (1860 and 1960). Not even their vice-presidents escaped this curious chain of coincidences, for both of them were Johnsons – Lincoln's was Andrew Johnson, Kennedy's was Lyndon Johnson.

Lincoln and Kennedy were clearly linked by fate – but, tragically, not by good fortune.

# Lost Worlds, Lasting Secrets

## NAZCA LINES

For the world's largest work of art to be also the world's least visible work of art may seem like a contradiction in terms. Yet the Nazca lines of Peru are both of these things, and more.

In September 1926, a team of archaeologists led by Professor Julio C. Tello was digging at Cantallo, near an expanse of desert in southern Peru called the Nazca Plain, when two of its members climbed a hill close by and made an extraordinary discovery. To their amazement, they saw that the desert at Nazca resembled the sketchbook of a giant, for it was intricately patterned with thousands of straight lines, curves, geometrical shapes and even various animal outlines. Yet all were of such enormous size that their shapes could be discerned only when viewed from above. At ground level, they simply resembled long shallow grooves, and even then could be perceived clearly only when observers stood astride them.

Consequently, the lines had hitherto been largely ignored. Indeed, as Stuart Gordon noted in *The Paranormal*, the Pan American Highway had been built through this desert region without anyone even noticing these designs. During the 1930s, however, the archaeologists' discovery was confirmed and expanded upon by accounts and

photographs obtained from Peruvian Air Force pilots flying over these fascinating patterns. The markings extend across about 1300 square kilometres (500 square miles) and are nowadays referred to as the Nazca lines. Pottery fragments found in association with them date their creation to somewhere between 300 BC and AD 540.

*On a vast scale, the complex designs in the Nazca lines are visible only from the air.*

The Nazca Plain is covered with dark stones, and its designs were created simply by selectively removing some of these stones, thereby exposing the paler yellowish-white soil beneath. In this way, the distinctive pale lines appear upon an otherwise dark surface. In other words, the actual nature of these lines is quite mundane; what makes them so astonishing is their extraordinary

accuracy, bearing in mind not only that their dimensions are colossal but also that their shapes can be recognised only from the air.

For instance, some of the straight lines are up to 8 kilometres (5 miles) long, yet on average they do not deviate more than 3 metres (10 feet) in every mile. Moreover, even though several of the designs are both enormous and extremely complex – portraying a variety of different animals, including a condor-like bird, a whale, a spider, even a hummingbird – when viewed from the air they are perfectly formed, with no distorted or otherwise inaccurate outlines.

How could such perfection be achieved? And what was the function of these enigmatic earthworks anyway? Such questions have preoccupied a generation of researchers captivated by "Nazca linealogy", foremost of whom is unquestionably Maria Reiche. This German mathematician has spent most of her life studying the Nazca lines, beginning in the 1940s with fellow devotee Professor Paul Kosok from Long Island University, New York, and continuing alone after his death in 1959. Kosok believed that the Nazca lines had astronomical significance, that they comprised a form of celestial calendar, and Reiche's researches supported his conclusion. Some of the lines seem to mark the seasonal appearance of various constellations, whereas certain others pin-point the locations of sunrise and sunset at the two equinoxes and the summer solstice. But was this their only purpose?

Many others have since been suggested. It is known that the Incas gained spiritual solace from walking along specially laid-out lines called ceques, so perhaps the Nazca people who long preceded them produced the Nazca lines in order to derive a similar benefit. Another popular explanation links the lines to irrigation and the identification of water sources. Alternatively, they could have been symbols of ownership or kinship, each line or series belonging to a different family, with the larger and more elaborate examples owned by the more important members of the community. As for the animal pictographs, these may have comprised nature and fertility symbols to be venerated accordingly, or perhaps they represented a form of art. Rather more imaginative ideas have sprung from the novel hypothesis that the lines

functioned as landing strips or refuelling centres for alien spacecraft.

As for the anomaly that their shapes can be appreciated only when viewed from the air, an American airline executive called Jim Woodman has come up with one line of conjecture. In 1975 he flew over the Nazca lines in a special hot-air balloon called *Condor I*, which he had purposefully constructed using materials that would have been available to the Nazca people. His aim was to demonstrate that they could have produced balloons for travelling over the desert, thus obtaining aerial views during their creation of the lines and thereby explaining the lines' amazing accuracy. Yet there is no independent evidence to support such a possibility, and other workers have shown that this accuracy could have been readily achieved using wholly terrestrial methods of marking out the lines with cord and sticks, and working from small-scale originals.

Perhaps the greatest wonder of the Nazca lines is that they have survived at all. This is due to a fluke

combination of favourable meteorology and biology. Even by desert standards, the Nazca region is extremely dry and there is very little wind, so erosion is not a problem, and vegetation is so sparse that the lines are in no danger of becoming overgrown.

✵

## EL DORADO

Led respectively by German explorer Nikolaus Federmann, Spanish conquistador Sebastian de Belalcazar, and Spanish explorer Gonzalo Jimenez de Quesada, three separate expeditions from Europe converged in 1539 upon a region of Colombia inhabited by the Chibcha people. Here Quesada was destined to found Bogotá, Colombia's present-day capital. However, the expeditions' principal goal then was to find a very different city – El Dorado, the fabled city of gold, spoken of by many South American peoples but hitherto undiscovered by the West.

Ironically, Quesada and company succeeded in their quest for El Dorado's identity, but without fully realizing it. They learnt that during the Chibchas' coronation ceremony, the new king was anointed with sticky earth followed by a liberal sprinkling of gold, thus coating him from head to foot in a gleaming gilded "skin". This was the real El Dorado – not a golden city, but a golden man. He would sit aboard a raft, placed upon the nearby Lake Guatavita and laden with resplendent golden gifts for the powerful god who supposedly inhabited this sacred lake. Once El Dorado had dropped his people's gifts into Guatavita's deep waters, he would immerse himself in the lake until his glittering covering had washed away – yielding a further tribute to the water deity – and then return to the shore to begin his reign.

Notwithstanding this revelation, some European explorers vainly continued to search for a wondrous golden city, spurred on by stories of Manoa – an idyllic magical island floating upon a great salt lake and brimming with golden artefacts of every kind. This wonderland has even been sought in modern times – its suggested

## THE GLOWING MUMMIES OF PERU

In a short account published by *Strange Magazine* in 1992, merchant seaman Curtis A. Rowlett recalled a recent conversation with a fellow sailor (identified only as J.P. in the periodical). The sailor claimed that in spring 1989, while awaiting repairs to his ship in Peru, he had met a local pilot with a very interesting tale to tell. According to the pilot, there was a mysterious cave near the Nazca Plain that contained five small mummies which glowed in the dark. Moreover, anyone who touched them developed strange open sores on their fingers. J.P. planned to visit this cave with the pilot and see the mummies for himself, but his ship's repairs were completed that same day, so he missed the opportunity to do so. Just a sailor's yarn – or yet another Nazca-related anomaly?

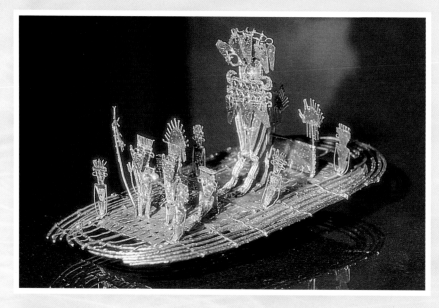

nineteenth century – and the departure of the Auroras! During the 1820s, a number of vessels visited their documented location, but the islands had vanished without trace. Their most celebrated seeker was the explorer Captain James Weddell, who diligently cruised back and forth in the vicinity plotted very precisely by Bustamente, but he failed to find them. Nevertheless, one or two claimed observations were made by other voyagers during later years, including a sighting in December 1856 by the brig *Helen Baird*, and what appears to be the anomalous Auroras' final bow, when two islands were spied in the correct area by Captain B.H. Hatfield aboard the *Gladys* in June 1892.

Another phantom of the Falklands is the Isla Grande, said to lie just north of the Auroras, along the forty-fifth parallel. It was first reported in 1675 by Antonio de la Roche, who also discovered South Georgia, but like its three southerly compatriots it has resisted all modern-day attempts to relocate it. Some researchers now dismiss it as nothing more than a poorly seen projection jutting out from the South American mainland.

Rather more difficult to explain away is the disappearance of an archipelago, as in the case of Davisland. This was the name given by cartographers to a group

*Above:*
*The real El Dorado was a "golden man" ceremony which installed new chiefs of the Chibcha people.*
*Left:*
*At the height of the ceremony the chief would dive, covered in gold dust, into the waters of Lake Guatavita.*

localities have included southern Surinam, south-eastern Venezuela and Brazil's Mato Grosso (proposed by lost explorer Lt-Col. Percy Fawcett) – but there is no more evidence for its reality than for a city of El Dorado.

sketched and even named them – New Island (the most northerly), Low Island (the central one) and Southernmost Island. In his survey, he noted that they were cold, dark and partly snow-covered.

Then came the arrival of the

## ✵ VANISHING ISLANDS

Islands that mysteriously vanish into thin air are commonplace in mythology and fairy tales, but quite a few true-life examples are also on record, particularly from South American waters. Of these, the most famous – or infamous, perhaps – are the Aurora Islands. This tantalizing trio reputedly lay midway between the Falkland Islands and South Georgia, and were first reported in 1762 by the whaler *Aurora*, though no one went ashore to explore them. Several other ships also recorded seeing them during the later years of the eighteenth century. In 1794, J. de Bustamente, captain of the Spanish corvette *Atrevida*, meticulously charted,

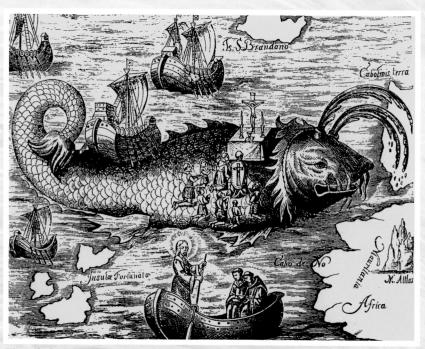

*The tribulations of terra firma: St Brendan is said to have mistaken a whale for an island, and landed on it.*

of islands of uncertain number sited about 800 kilometres (500 miles) west of Chile and reported in 1687 by Captain John Davis and his crew. Yet despite repeated searches, no one else ever found them.

Nevertheless, during one such search, by the Dutch Admiral Roggeveen, a very significant discovery *was* made: this was Easter Island, and its enigmatic giant statues (pp. 41–43), spotted on Easter Sunday 1722. An intriguing link between this island and vanished Davisland has been proposed by archaeologist Professor J. MacMillan Brown, who speculated that Easter Island was the sacred cemetery of the unknown inhabitants of Davisland. However, as this latter chain of islands appears to be permanently lost, it is unlikely that his idea can be pursued further.

Another phantom island reported in Easter Island's general vicinity is Podesta, as well as an unnamed isle spied by the S.S. *Glewalon* in 1912, and yet another, Sarah Ann Island, recorded far to the west of Ecuador. None can be found today. Nor can the St Vincent Islands (not to be confused with the single Caribbean island of St Vincent), which were discovered off Panama's west coast by Antonio Martinus in 1789, and inhabited for a time not long afterwards by Father Santa Clara, a Californian priest. Also worth noting is the evanescent Island of Brasil, if only to point out that despite its name, it shares no geographical link with Brazil. Instead, its rare appearances occur off the west coast of Ireland!

✦

# LT-COL. PERCY FAWCETT – AN EXPLORER LOST IN GREEN HELL

On 20 April 1925, at the onset of what proved to be his final, ill-fated expedition in Brazil's Mato Grosso, British explorer and soldier Lieutenant-Colonel Percy Harrison Fawcett relayed

*Lieutenant-Colonel Percy Harrison Fawcett, British explorer and soldier.*

the following message to London by the Overland Brazilian Telegraph in Rondonia:

*I have but one object: to bare the mysteries that the jungle fastnesses of South America have concealed for so many centuries. We are encouraged in our hope of finding the ruins of an ancient, white civilisation and the degenerate offspring of a once cultivated race.*

On 29 May, 57-year-old Fawcett

reported his position (Lat. 11° 43' S; Long. 54° 35' W) at Dead Horse Camp in the Xingú Basin to the North American Newspaper Alliance funding his foray, and signed off by saying, "You need have no fear of any failure". Those were the last words ever received from him by the outside world. After marching boldly into the jaws of the Mato Grosso's green hell, his three-man party was entirely engulfed by it.

Even as a youth, Fawcett had been obsessed by the idea that ancient cities far older than the Egyptian civilization

*The Mato Grosso, a vast impenetrable land which still holds the secret of Fawcett's lost expedition.*

awaited discovery in untraversed parts of the world, particularly South America. He also believed that the legendary continent of Atlantis had really existed. Weaving these strands together, and supplementing them with information gathered from the many indigenous peoples that he had encountered during several explorations of South America's verdant interior, he formulated the notion that if such cities could be found, they would surely be the relics of an advanced white race that had fled from the doomed Atlantis before it sank beneath the ocean waves and had settled in the forests of South America. Here, Fawcett believed, the Atlanteans had survived, but their society had ultimately degenerated. Eventually, only the stony husks of their once-magnificent temples and palaces remained, still illuminated by everlasting globes of light – the last vestige of the Atlanteans' highly sophisticated scientific accomplishments.

In Rio de Janeiro, Fawcett had found an old Portuguese report of the forgotten discovery in 1753 of the ruins of a stone city, enclosed by a wall, deep in the Mato Grosso. And on 20 April 1925, accompanied by his son Jack, aged 21, and a cameraman called Raleigh Rimell, he set out on his ill-fated expedition from Cuyaba to relocate this city and prove its Atlantean connections.

Since the disappearance of Fawcett's party, several teams have attempted to trace their footsteps, and a welter of contradictory stories have emerged. Some eyewitnesses claimed that they had seen the three men living with various indigenous peoples several years after their disappearance. During the 1930s and 1940s, a half-white, blue-eyed Kuikuro Indian boy called Dulipe was even said by some to be Jack's son by an Indian wife. In 1952, however, Dulipe was exposed as a freak partial albino, wholly unrelated to Jack and the innocent victim of a journalistic hoax.

In August 1946, explorer Orlando Vilas Boas tape-recorded a supposed confession by the chief of the Kalapalos Indians that his people had killed all three men – a claim substantiated five years later by the supposed discovery of Fawcett's skeleton in their territory. According to Miriam Tildesley, however, who examined the skeleton, it seemed to be at least a hundred years old, and

# THE MYSTERY OF THE MELTING ROCKS

Archaeologists in Latin America have often speculated upon the techniques responsible for the fine precision with which the huge stones used in constructing these lands' ancient cities were carved, given the stones' remarkably tight fit against one another. Although most experts believe that relatively ordinary procedures would have achieved this result, there is a possibility that one quite extraordinary technique also played its part.

Since the early 1980s, French polymer chemist Dr Joseph Davidovits has been researching the startling prospect that some ancient civilizations, including the creators of the Bolivian city of Tiahuanaco (pp.174–5), had developed a process by which crushed rock could be melted, moulded into a given shape (such as a huge cube or an elaborate statue) and then hardened to yield the required object. This would eliminate the laborious task of precision-carving solid blocks of rock into stone cubes for constructing buildings, or into ornamental sculptures.

*The fortress of Sacsayhuamán. Did the Incas have the technology to melt rocks?*

Davidovits claims that even today witch-doctors in Bolivia are known to powder rock, add natural chemicals to break it down, and then mould the slurry into amulets of solid stone. He has also successfully created his own synthetic rock or geopolymer that can be melted, shaped, then rehardened. His laboratory contains several shelves groaning under the weight of statues moulded from artificial rock, but most archaeologists remain unconvinced.

Testimony for the "melting" theory was also recorded by Professor Hiram Bingham, during his Peruvian expeditions that culminated in his sensational discovery of the lost Incan city of Machu Picchu in 1911. Bingham recounted stories by the local peoples about a special plant whose juices melted rock, enabling it to be worked into tightly fitted masonry.

In *"Things"*, Ivan T. Sanderson included data on this subject collected by Lt-Col. Percy Fawcett. One item concerned a man who had trekked 8 kilometres (5 miles) through virgin forest along the Pyrene River in the Peruvian province of Chuncho, only to discover at the end of his trek that his metal spurs had been corroded away. He mentioned this to his host, a local rancher, who asked if he had walked through a dense patch of plants with red fleshy leaves, growing about 15 cm (1 foot) high. When the man told him that he had, his host informed him that these were to blame, and were "the stuff the Incas used for shaping stones".

whereas Fawcett had long ago lost two teeth in his upper jaw during a vigorous football match, the upper jaw of the skeleton's skull still possessed both of them.

Somewhere in the Mato Grosso is the secret of Fawcett's disappearance, but this vast land is so impenetrable even today that there is little chance of ever uncovering the truth.

# Monstrous Mysteries

## Loys's Ape and Other Neotropical Man-beasts

Officially, South America has no apes. This is why the extraordinary creature depicted in an excellent photograph taken by a geologist while exploring this continent is so controversial.

Its story began one day in 1920, while Swiss geologist Dr François de Loys was leading an expedition through the rainforest on the border between Venezuela and Colombia. Suddenly, two strange ape-like creatures stepped out of some bushes just ahead of them, walking on their hind legs, lacking tails and standing approximately 1.5 metres (5 feet) tall. The creatures seemed greatly angered by the sight of the geologists and moved closer, as if to attack them. In order to protect themselves, the geologists had no option but to shoot at these animals, killing one of them, which proved to be a female. The other, presumably a male, turned and fled.

Unable to identify the large ape-like primate, and equally unable to carry its heavy body very far, they propped it into a sitting posture on a wooden crate,

placing a pole beneath its chin to keep it upright, and photographed it. Tragically, most of the photos were later lost when the geologists' boat capsized while they were travelling down a river, but one first-class picture did survive and is

*Loys's ape: officially there are no apes in South America.*

reproduced here. Some time after the expedition's return to Europe, Loys published an account of the strange ape-men in an *Illustrated London News* article (15 June 1929). This included the photo and it astounded the scientific world.

One French zoologist, Professor

George Montandon, was convinced that it depicted a genuine species of South American ape, the first ever known, which he formally christened *Ameranthropoides loysi* ("Loys's American ape"), but others were more sceptical. As the creature bore an overall resemblance to the familiar spider monkeys, they concluded that this is what it was, despite its much greater size, more robust body and dissimilar dentition (Loys claimed that it had fewer teeth than all known species of spider monkey). They even disputed Loys's statement that it was tailless, and suggested that he may have deliberately cut off or hidden its tail when photographing the animal, to make it look more like an ape.

Today, Loys's ape is virtually forgotten outside cryptozoological circles. Yet the existence of such creatures is apparently well known to the native people in many parts of Central and South America, who call them by a variety of different local names, including the shiru (Colombia), sisimite (Belize), vasitri (Venezuela), didi (Guyana), xipe (Nicaragua) and tarma (Peru). Certainly, there is no good evolutionary reason why the South American primates should not have given rise to an ape-like form equivalent to the Old World anthropoids.

In 1987, mycologist Gary Samuels from the New York Botanical Gardens

*Some zoologists dismissed Loys's ape as the spider monkey* ATELES PANISCUS.

was kneeling down on a forest floor in Guyana when he looked up to see a hairy 1.5-metre- (5-foot) tall ape-man walking by on its hind legs, apparently unaware of Samuels's presence, crouched on the ground. As it walked it uttered an occasional "hoo" cry. This was presumably a didi.

A rare opportunity to obtain the skeleton of a similar creature may have been lost in 1968. This was when a xipe was allegedly trapped in a cave by a group of Nicaraguan peasants, who then set fire to the bushes around it. It is claimed that they found its scorched skeleton inside the cave afterwards, but no one seems to have preserved it.

What *is* preserved, however, at Chicago's Field Museum of Natural History, is a distinctly ape-like "mask", carved in stone by the Guetar Indians of Costa Rica (AD 1200–1500). And statues

of gorilla-like entities have been discovered amid ruined cities half-hidden beneath the foliage in the rainforests of Central and South America.

No less interesting than accounts of elusive ape-men is the possible existence in South America of an undiscovered giant monkey. Reports collected by on-site zoologist Dr Peter Hocking from several different Indian tribes suggest that the forests of Peru conceal a monkey the size of a chimpanzee but with a very short tail and a face like a baboon. According to local people, it is known as the isnachi and is very rare, but is in any case avoided whenever possible because of its ferocity. One of its most characteristic activities is to rip apart the tops of chonta palm trees in order to procure the tender vegetable matter inside. This means that its presence within a given locality can be swiftly confirmed merely by finding trees damaged in this way, because no other creature is strong enough to do this.

Most mysterious of all are the alux, reported from the Yucatán Peninsula in Mexico. The males are described as dwarf-sized humanoids with jet-black beards and clad in a dress-like garment, known as a hupile, worn by the mysterious Mayas. Occasionally, female alux are also seen, with very long dark hair and wearing a similar garment to the males.

Late one evening in 1977, a bearded 1-metre- (3-foot) tall alux was seen in the ancient walled city of Mayapán (the Mayas' former capital) by the city's current caretaker, a young modern-day Mayan called Xuc. The alux had a disproportionately large head and was wearing a hupile and carrying a large machete over its shoulder. As Xuc drew nearer, however, the angry alux bombarded him with a barrage of small clay pellets before disappearing into the shadows of the night.

Interestingly, investigator Bill Mack has noted that many ruined Mayan temples in Yucatán are fronted by one or more tiny stone "houses" with doorways less than a metre (3 feet) high. According to orthodox science, these odd structures are votary shrines, but the modern-day Mayas claim that they were the homes of favoured alux.

# WILDLIFE OF THE WEIRD, BUT VERY WONDERFUL, VARIETY

Some of the strangest but potentially most sensational mystery animals on record have been reported from the secluded rainforests, mountains and rivers of South America.

For many years, zoologist Dr David Oren from the Goeldi Museum in Brazil has been following up local reports from the dense Mato Grosso region of Amazonia in his longstanding search for an exceedingly odd creature called the mapinguary. According to the local Indians, it has red fur and when squatting on its hind legs is as tall as a man; it leaves strange footprints that seem to be back-to-front and faecal droppings similar to those of horses; it emits loud shouting cries and is said to be invulnerable to bullets.

Dr Oren feels that this description closely matches that of an officially extinct ground-living sloth called a mylodontid. This is known to science not only from fossils and preserved faecal droppings (which are indeed horse-like), but also from some remarkable mummified individuals several millennia old, yet still covered with reddish-brown fur. From these specimens, zoologists know that mylodontids had bony nodules in their skin that would have served as effective body armour (perhaps explaining the mapinguary's invulnerability).

The Indians also claim that the mapinguary has an extra mouth, in the centre of its belly, and that, when threatened, it releases a hideous stench that suffocates its attackers. This may sound quite bizarre, but Oren suggests that these descriptions might simply refer to some form of gas-secreting gland, used for defence. If one day he finds a mapinguary, it could well prove to be the largest living mammal native to South America; and if it really is a ground sloth, it will resurrect from extinction one of the most peculiar

*Claims that this mysterious pelt (held here by cryptozoologist Dennis Vrettos) comes from a hitherto-unknown species of wolf remain controversial.*

Lorenz Hagenbeck was visiting a market in Buenos Aires when he saw a very unusual dog pelt for sale. Although somewhat reminiscent of the maned wolf's fur, with a very dense mane-like covering over its neck, it was much longer, thicker and darker over the body, as seen here in this previously unpublished photograph. Its colour graded from black on the upper parts to dark brown on the neck and under parts, and its ears were much smaller and rounder than those of the maned wolf.

Learning that this strange pelt was from a mysterious form of dog reputedly native to the Andes (and noticing that three other pelts just like it were also for sale at this market), Hagenbeck purchased it. When it was subsequently examined by German scientists they concluded that it seemed to be a hitherto-unknown, mountain-dwelling equivalent of the maned wolf. One of these scientists, pioneering cryptozoologist Dr Ingo Krumbiegel, also found a strange canine skull of Andean origin that may have come from such a beast. In 1949, based upon the skull and the skin, he published a formal description of this elusive maned wolf of the mountains, calling it the Andean wolf *Oreocyon* (since changed to *Dasycyon*) *hagenbecki*.

No further skins or skeletal remains were obtained, however, and in later years hair analyses were conducted that pointed towards a domestic sheepdog as a possible identity (or at least as an ancestor) for the Andean wolf. Yet with the recent development of comparative

groups of mammals ever known. A similar beast, locally termed the ellengassen, has also been described from Patagonia.

Equally extraordinary is the minhocão, a huge worm-like beast said to be 23 metres (75 feet) long (but this is no doubt an exaggeration), with black scaly skin and two tentacle-like structures on its head. Reported from Uruguay and Paraná, southern Brazil, this grotesque creature spends much of its time underground. However, its existence is readily betrayed by the dramatic effects of its stupendous subterranean excavations, which will often cause the sudden collapse of hillsides and roads, and are sometimes deep enough to divert the course of rivers.

Zoologists have previously attempted, very unsatisfactorily, to identify the minhocão as an undiscovered species of enormous lungfish, or even a surviving glyptodont – an immense armadillo-like mammal believed to have died out at least 10,000 years ago. As I discussed in my book *In Search of Prehistoric Survivors*, however, a much more compatible identity for it is a gigantic form of caecilian – a limbless worm-like amphibian of subterranean, burrowing life-style. These creatures are already represented in South America by several modest-sized species, some of which do indeed have scaly skin and a pair of tentacles on their head.

Greatly resembling a fiery-furred fox on stilts, the maned wolf *Chrysocyon brachyurus* is native to the Patagonian pampas. Officially, this extremely distinctive animal has no particularly close relatives among other species of wild dog – or has it?

In 1927, German animal dealer

*The minhocão may be a gigantic form of caecilian (*HYPOGEOPHIS ROSTRATA*).*

DNA techniques it is surely time now to re-examine this tantalizing pelt, to determine conclusively whether *Dasycyon hagenbecki* is actually a wolf in sheepdog's clothing after all.

No less mysterious is the maipolina of the Maroni River at Maripasoula, Guyana. A greatly feared beast that supposedly inhabits caves and hollows in the river bank, it is said to be about 3 metres (10 feet) long, with short fur that is fawn in colour on top (plus a paler dorsal stripe) and whitish underneath, large eyes, drooping ears, clawed feet, a cow-like tail, and – most noticeable of all – a pair of huge tusks resembling those of a walrus. Attempts have been made to equate this animal with a giant form of otter, but these are frustrated by its incongruous tusks and also by its cow-like (hence tufted?) tail and drooping ears.

Another walrus-lookalike, but with shaggy yellow fur, has been reported from the rivers of Paraguay, where it is termed the yaquaru or water tiger. Interestingly, similar creatures have been described from tropical rivers in central Africa too, and cryptozoologist Dr Bernard Heuvelmans has boldly postulated that these may be surviving sabre-tooth tigers specialized for an amphibious existence. In South America, normal terrestrial sabre-tooths certainly survived up to around 10,000 years ago. Could some still exist here today, but adapted for an aquatic life-style as suggested by Heuvelmans for the African mystery beasts? South America evidently has ample surprises still in store for any real-life Professor Challengers.

# BOTANY OF THE BIZARRE

A botanical monster capable of devouring animals and even human beings has been reported from parts of Central America. In an issue of *Sea and Land* from 1887, J.W. Buel called it the ya-te-veo tree, and described it as having a short thick trunk with immense spine-like shoots at its summit that bear dagger-shaped

*The Venus flytrap (DIONAEA MUSCIPULA) has a reassuringly modest appetite.*

thorns along their edges. These shoots hang down to the ground and appear lifeless, until an unwary person walks between them, towards the trunk itself. Then, without warning, the shoots rise up and entwine themselves around him, pressing him on to the trunk's surface where they instantly impale him with their long thorns and crush him until his body is drained of blood, which is rapidly absorbed through the tree's surface. This is just one of several controversial meat-eating plants reported from tropical America but whose reality remains unverified.

On 27 August 1892, for example, the *Illustrated London News* reported a dog-devouring tree in Nicaragua. Apparently, a naturalist called Dunstan had been seeking plant specimens in swamps surrounding Lake Nicaragua when he heard his dog cry out in agony. Running to his assistance, Dunstan found to his horror that the dog was enmeshed in a fine network of rope-like roots and fibres, comprising a bizarre type of vine, almost black in colour and secreting a thick sticky gum. Only with very great difficulty did Dunstan succeed in cutting through the vine's clinging fibres to release his dog, and after he had done so he saw that the animal's skin was covered in sucker marks, where the vine had seemingly pierced its flesh and sucked its blood. The natives knew this macabre species well, and told Dunstan that it could drain the nourishment from a large lump of meat in as little as five minutes.

A comparable form, referred to locally as the snake-tree, has supposedly been recorded from an outlying spur of Mexico's Sierra Madre. According to the claims of a traveller who came across it during the late nineteenth century, a bird that perched on one of its branches was immediately seized by it and crushed, its blood being absorbed

through the plant's surface until its corpse was dry. After watching this grisly spectacle, the traveller rashly touched one of its branches: the branch immediately closed upon his hand, and with such force that he tore his skin when wrenching his hand away!

What may well have been the same, still-unrecognized species was encountered by the famous French explorer Byron de Prorok in early 1933, when he led an expedition into the almost impenetrable jungle region of the Chiapas, in southern Mexico. Just two hours after first entering the forest, their guide, Domingo, pointed to a huge plant and when de Prorok looked at it closely he saw to his astonishment that the plant had captured a bird. This had alighted upon one of the leaves, which had promptly closed, its thorns penetrating the bird's body. Domingo referred to this deadly species as the "plante vampire".

Even more recently, during the early 1970s, Brazilian explorer Mariano da Silva came upon a particularly dramatic flesh-eater of the floral variety while searching for a settlement of Yatapu people on the Brazilian border with Guyana. This species allegedly releases a very distinctive scent that is particularly attractive to monkeys, luring them to it and enticing them to climb its trunk –

*Evading vicious vines is the stuff of derring-do. This illustration accompanied 'The Purple Terror' by Fred M. White in* **Strand Magazine**, *September 1899.*

whereupon its leaves totally envelop them, rendering these hapless creatures invisible and inaudible to anyone witnessing this vile spectacle. Three days or so later, the leaves open again, and from them drop the bones of their victims, from which every vestige of flesh has been stripped. This resembles the activity of a giant-sized Venus flytrap, but so far science has still to receive a specimen for examination.

# ✸ GIANT ANACONDAS

For many years, the longest reliably reported anaconda *Eunectes murinus* on record was deemed to be an 11.5-metre-(37½-foot) specimen killed by petroleum geologist Robert Lamon while leading a party exploring for oil in the llanos of the upper Orinoco River in eastern Colombia; it was documented in 1944 by herpetologist Dr Emmett R. Dunn from Haverford College, Pennsylvania. In a *Bulletin of the Chicago Herpetological Society* paper for September 1993, however, zoologists Dr Raymond Gilmore and Dr John Murphy revealed that this snake had actually measured only a little over 7 metres (24 feet), indicating that Dunn's report had been in error.

Yet even if this specimen had truly measured 11.5 metres, it would still have been effortlessly overshadowed by certain others reported over the years, especially from parts of Amazonia. Here, colossal anacondas far greater in size than any officially verified by science are so well known to the local people that they have even been given their own specific name – the sucuriju gigante.

One of these outsized snakes was encountered in 1907 by Lt-Col. Percy Fawcett (see pp. 20–21) while he and his expedition were voyaging along the Rio Abunã close to its confluence with the Rio Negro, near the southern border of western Brazil. Without warning, the triangular head of an immense anaconda, followed by several feet of its undulating body, surfaced almost under the bow of his canoe and began to

emerge on to the river bank.

Fawcett immediately shot the creature, killing it outright, then went ashore to examine its carcass. This, he claimed, was of prodigious length: "As far as it was possible to measure, a length of forty-five feet lay out of the water, and seventeen feet in it, making a total length of sixty-two feet." He also noted that the Araguaya and Tocantíns swamps harbour a huge black version, known as the dormidera ("sleeper") after the loud snoring noise that it makes.

Even more enormous was the monstrous specimen that slithered ashore in 1948 and secreted itself amid Fort Tabatinga's fortifications on the River Oiapoc in the Guaporé territory. According to a report in a Rio de Janeiro newspaper, which also featured a photo of the snake, it measured a stupendous 35 metres (115 feet), and a team of soldiers sent to dispatch it fired at least 500 machine-gun bullets into its

body before it was killed. Tragically for science, its gargantuan carcase was rapidly pushed back into the river afterwards.

As an added distinction, some Guyanan giant anacondas are said to be horned too, and these specimens are called camoodi by the locals.

Biomechanically speaking, gigantic anacondas are not impossible, because their great weight would be effectively buoyed as long as they remained in the water. Moreover, many extra-large anaconda skins have been formally documented, but as snake skins can be easily stretched, these are unreliable sources of evidence for the reality of such creatures. In contrast, there are still many reports of living giant anacondas that cannot be dismissed quite so readily (even when we have excluded evident hoaxes and exaggerated estimations of size). After all, an anaconda skin cannot be stretched while the anaconda is still in it!

*Fortunately, when Lt-Col. Percy Fawcett encountered a gigantic anaconda under similar circumstances, he was rather better prepared.*

# Tropical Magic

## THE CRYSTAL SKULLS OF DOOM

One day in 1927, teenager Anna Mitchell-Hedges was assisting her adoptive father, a British explorer called F.A. "Mike" Mitchell-Hedges, in his excavations at the ruined Mayan city of Lubantum in British Honduras (now Belize), when she made a momentous discovery. Digging in a temple, she spied something shining beneath its altar. It proved to be a life-sized model of a human skull, meticulously sculpted from a lump of pure quartz rock crystal. The lower jaw was missing, but three months later this was also found by Anna, buried just a metre or more away from the skull's hiding place. Thus reads the official history of what is variously termed the Mitchell-Hedges crystal skull or the Skull of Doom – and what is deemed by many to be the most astounding work of art ever created by human hand.

This fascinating artefact has been in Anna's ownership ever since she discovered it; but it is not unique. A second life-sized skull hewn from rock crystal is also on record: this one has been owned since 1898 by the Museum of Mankind in London (part of the British Museum), which purchased it from Tiffany's, the famous New York jewellers, for £120.

The craftsmanship of these two skulls is truly exemplary. After comparing their respective measurements with those of a real human skull, in July 1936 eminent British anthropologist Dr G.M. Morant documented his findings in the scientific journal *Man*, commenting:

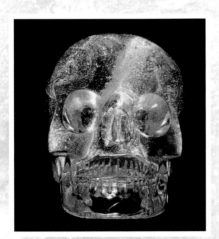

*The two crystal skulls of doom are thought to be related. This one is held by the Museum of Mankind in London.*

*Not one of these measurements would be at all exceptional for an actual skull except the orbital index ... which appears to be slightly removed from the human range for this character. At the same time the other measurements are in remarkably close accordance.*

When the two crystal skulls are directly compared with each other, however, certain differences can be perceived. Whereas the lower jaw of the Museum of Mankind's skull is an intrinsic component of this sculpture, the Mitchell-Hedges skull's lower jaw was fashioned as a separate item, which can be moved up and down when fitted to the skull. Leading on from this difference, the Museum skull is more stylized in form, whereas the Mitchell-Hedges skull is much closer to a naturalistic anatomical rendering.

Indeed, this latter specimen corresponds so precisely with the genuine article that when illuminated by radiant sunlight it is as if the bony substance of a real human skull has been magically vitrified, transformed into crystalline fire. Most spectacular of all, however, are its prismatic eyes, which are so skilfully fashioned that they effectively concentrate light in a manner that imparts an uncanny luminescence throughout the entire skull. Yet none of its glistening surfaces betrays even the vaguest hint of how this astonishing artefact was manufactured. In contrast, one of the teeth of the Museum skull bears what may be a slight mark made by a powered cutter.

In his paper, Morant claimed that it was "impossible to avoid the conclusion that the crystal skulls are not of independent origin ... it is safe to conclude that they are representations of the same human skull [quite possibly a female specimen], though one may have been copied from the other". If so, he considered it likeliest that the less precise Museum skull had been copied from the more finely detailed Mitchell-Hedges skull.

Perhaps only marginally less remarkable a wonder than the skulls themselves is our extraordinary dearth of knowledge concerning their origins, the identities of those who fashioned them, and the possible functions of such mesmerisingly macabre effigies. To begin with, much doubt has been publicly aired by several researchers concerning the circumstances surrounding Anna Mitchell-Hedges's alleged discovery of the crystal skull at Lubantum. Pointing out that the day she found it just so happened to be her seventeenth birthday, they have speculated that her father may have deliberately planted the skull for her to find, as a birthday surprise. Yet if this is true, where did he obtain it?

On 15 September 1943, the skull was put up for auction at Sotheby's in London by Sydney Burney, a local art dealer. It did not reach its reserve price, however, and Anna's father bought it for £400. He later claimed that some time *before* the auction he had given it to Burney as security on a loan, and thus by purchasing it at the auction he was merely redeeming what already belonged to him. Sceptics, however, point out that Morant's paper, published seven years before the auction, referred to this skull as "the Burney skull", and did not mention Mitchell-Hedges. Is it possible, therefore, that the story of Anna's finding of the skull at Lubantum is a fabrication on the part of her father (whose fondness for story-telling was widely known), and that the skull had first come into the ownership of the Mitchell-Hedges family only when it was bought from Burney at the auction by Anna's father?

According to gemmologist G.F. Kunz, the second crystal skull had been brought from Mexico to Europe by a Spanish officer some time before France's occupation of Mexico in the mid 1860s, and was sold to an English

collector. When he died, it changed owners several times until it was purchased by Tiffany's and thence by the British Museum.

In his autobiography *Danger My Ally*, Anna's father claimed that the "Skull of Doom" was "at least 3,600 years old and according to legend was used by the high priest of the Maya when performing esoteric rites. It is said that when he willed death with the help of the skull, death invariably followed. It has been described as the embodiment of all evil." In their book, *The Mayan Prophecies*, Adrian G. Gilbert and Maurice M. Cotterell proffered the evocative suggestion that this skull may have been used by the high priest as an elaborate burning glass in the Mayan fire ceremony. They proposed that if the priest held its exactly carved form at a certain angle to the sun, it would act like a lens, emitting a bright tongue of fire via the refraction of sunlight through its opened mouth. Perhaps this explains its mobile lower jaw.

As for the Museum skull, anthropologist H.J. Braunholtz asserted in 1936 that its stylized form, with circular eye sockets and ill-defined teeth, was typical of late Aztec art.

More recently, however, several other possible sources for the rock crystal used in the skulls' manufacture have been put forward, including Brazil, Cavalaveras County in California, and Peru. In addition, the skulls may actually have been manufactured rather more recently than originally assumed, and far away from whatever source of rock crystal was used: Japan, Qing Dynasty China, and even Renaissance Europe have been proposed as likely possibilities.

Of the two crystal skulls, the Mitchell-Hedges specimen has inspired the greater public fascination, for according to crystal expert Frank Dorland, who studied it for six years, it is uniquely associated with some very bizarre reports and phenomena. As summarized in Time-Life's lavish volume *Feats and Wisdom of the Ancients*, Dorland claimed that this skull:

*... sometimes changed color or filled with a cottony haze; that it produced an "elusive perfume" and strange tinkling*

*sounds; that images of mountains, temples, and other objects appeared within it; and that an aura once surrounded it for several minutes.*

Others who saw the skull while it was on loan to Dorland reported similar phenomena. Some observers even attested that while they were gazing at it, their pulse quickened, their arm and leg muscles tightened, and their eyes were physically tugged in their sockets. Dorland believes that these effects are not physical but hallucinatory, somehow triggered by the skull's crystal structure. It is little wonder indeed that it is called the Skull of Doom.

✵

# THE GIANT STONE BALLS OF COSTA RICA

Like the scene of an unfinished game of marbles played by a long-vanished race of Titans, the Diquís Delta of Costa Rica is liberally strewn with an array of stone orbs. Known as Las Bolas Grandes ("The Giant Balls"), numbering well over a thousand in total and occurring in association with pre-Columbian artefacts, some of these granitic globes are only a few centimetres in diameter, but many are colossal – up to 2.5 metres (8 feet) across and weighing more than 16 tonnes.

Yet their very existence remained unknown to the outside world until the 1930s, when the dense vegetation covering the delta was levelled in order to establish banana plantations here and its secret spheres were finally exposed. Six decades have passed by since then, but science is still unable to explain how these giant orbs were created – by humankind or by nature?

They have been extensively studied by several archaeologists, notably Dr Samuel Lothrop from the Peabody Museum at Harvard University, and everyone has marvelled at their near-perfect spherical shape, regardless of size. One of the largest balls, with a diameter of 2 metres (6½ feet), deviates in its circumference by only 1.27 cm

*Dr Samuel Lothrop made extensive studies of Las Bolas Grandes following their discovery in the 1930s. This is one of his photographs, showing the balls in their original location.*

or $^1/_2$ inch (i.e. approximately two-tenths of 1 per cent). Yet the identity of the long-vanished sculptors responsible for precision stone carving of such an exceptionally high standard as this remains a mystery.

Nowadays, the general consensus of opinion is that the Bolas Grandes embody a canny combination of human and natural design. Great quantities of geometrically accurate stone spheres measuring up to 3.3 metres (11 feet) in diameter yet derived from wholly natural, volcanic processes have been discovered in Mexico. Although they lack the professional external finish displayed by the Costa Rican balls, these Mexican examples eloquently demonstrate that Mother Nature is capable of some impressive feats of mechanical engineering.

Also relevant to this line of speculation is the fact that the granite from which the Costa Rican balls are carved is not indigenous to the Diquís Delta. Hence their raw material clearly originated from elsewhere; yet there is no evidence to suggest that the nearest

*The balls vary in size. Some are smaller than footballs, others more than 2 metres (6$^1/_2$ feet) across.*

source (and even that is many kilometres away) has ever been quarried. At present, therefore, the origin of their stony substance is yet another mystery associated with these giant orbs.

Taking all this into account, researchers consider it likely not only that Costa Rica's nameless sculptors

were inspired by natural spheres comparable to those of Mexico, but also that some such spheres were imported from foreign parts to the Diquís Delta. There they were directly used by these artisans, improving upon nature's originals to produce the mathematically precise, expertly surfaced versions that we now know as the Bolas Grandes.

Even if all this is true, however, we have still to explain *why* they carved these balls. What was their function – indicatory, symbolic? Perhaps we are looking too deeply for answers: is it too heretical or unscientific to suggest that they were wantonly ornamental?

## ✴ ZOMBIES

Belief in zombies – the living dead – is widespread throughout the voodoo-ridden West Indian country of Haiti, on the island of Hispaniola, to such an extent that even the poorest peasants willingly pay large sums of money for heavy slabs of stone to be placed over their relatives' graves. This is to prevent their corpses from being stolen by evil sorcerers, called bokors, who magically restore them to an eerie half-life as zombies and then take them to remote areas where they are put to work as slaves. Although they can eat, breathe and move, zombies are incapable of thinking for themselves, and have no knowledge of who they once were or of anything else concerning their previous life.

All of this sounds like something from a cheap horror movie, but there are dozens of confirmed cases of zombies and zombification on file, spanning countless years. In 1980, for example, a police officer saw a female zombie ambling mindlessly through a village under his supervision, and recognized her as Natagette Joseph – a woman whom he had pronounced dead in 1966, when she was aged about 46.

Back in October 1936, an almost naked female zombie was found wandering close to a roadway in Haiti's Artibonite Valley. After being transferred to the authorities, she was formally identified by her father and her brother as Felicia Felix-Mentor, who had died from a quick-acting fever in 1907 and had been buried. What makes this case so interesting is that it was the first to feature a Western investigator.

While under surveillance at the hospital at Gonaives, Felicia was visited by the American ethnographer Zora Neale Hurston, who photographed and studied her closely during the visit.

*"That blank face with the dead eyes..." American ethnographer Zora Neale Hurston took this photograph of zombified Felicia Felix-Mentor in Haiti in 1937.*

Hurston was later to record: "The sight was dreadful. That blank face with the dead eyes. The eyelids were white all around the eyes as if they had been burned with acid. There was nothing you could say to her or get from her except by looking at her, and the sight of this wreckage was too much to endure for long."

By far the most celebrated of all zombie cases, however, is that of Clairvius Narcisse – the only zombie to become a television star! One day in 1980, Angelina Narcisse was shopping in the market-place of l'Estère, her home village, when suddenly a voice whispered into her ear the boyhood nickname of her long-dead brother Clairvius. He had died from fever on 2 May 1962 at the Albert Schweitzer Hospital, Deschapelles in the Artibonite Valley, and had been buried the next day at a cemetery north of l'Estère. Bearing in mind that his nickname was known only to immediate members of their family, and had not even been used by any of them since childhood, Angelina was naturally startled to hear it. She was far more startled, however, when she turned round to see who had uttered it – for there, albeit a little shaky on his feet and somewhat bleary-eyed, stood Clairvius!

Not surprisingly, Angelina promptly fainted, but after recovering she confirmed that it was indeed her supposedly dead brother. His identity was also verified by other members of their family, by over 200 l'Estère residents and by his ability to answer correctly many detailed questions about his boyhood that would have baffled everyone but the real Clairvius.

This extraordinary episode attracted such widespread media interest that even the BBC arrived from Britain and made a television film about it. But most important of all, here was a zombie that, unlike others previously investigated, was still sufficiently alert and articulate to be able to reveal how he had actually become a zombie, and what had happened to him afterwards.

It turned out that he had fathered many illegitimate children but had refused to provide financial support for them, and he had also argued violently with his brother over a land dispute. As a result, his brother had hired a bokor to zombify Clairvius. This had been achieved by surreptitiously feeding him a secret poison that had initially produced fever-like symptoms but soon sent him into a death-like trance, in which he was fully conscious yet wholly paralysed, with ghostly skin pallor and a near-imperceptible heartbeat. Even when examined by two different doctors he appeared to be dead, and so he was buried – alive!

Not long afterwards, his body, still paralysed, was dug up by the bokor, who gave him a second type of drug that rendered him sluggishly mobile but prevented any type of clear, decisive thought. Once this had been administered, Clairvius was savagely beaten and was then taken away to the north of Haiti, where he spent the next two years as a slave, working alongside other zombies and constantly abused by their sadistic sorcerer master. He might never have escaped, but one day another zombie somehow awoke sufficiently to attack and kill the bokor. Once the bokor was dead, their periodic intake of the mind-controlling drug ceased, and in the case of Clairvius he gradually began to remember who he was and what had taken place. During the following years, he roamed from one region to another, but after

learning that his brother had died he returned to l'Estère, where he met his sister Angelina.

This astonishing account was of keen interest to American biologist Wade Davis, working at that time in the Harvard Botanical Museum, who was eager to uncover the biochemical identities of the mysterious substances used in zombification – immobilizing, then reviving and brainwashing those victims selected by bokors for this purpose. After visiting Haiti to research the subject and to collect samples of the substances, Davis ascertained that the immobilizing poison contained two very noteworthy constituents. One was tetrodotoxin, a very effective nerve poison inducing rapid, profound paralysis, and commonly obtained from puffer fishes. The other was a fluid containing a potent anaesthetic and hallucinogen, secreted by the skin glands of the highly poisonous cane toad *Bufo marinus*. Davis has recounted his findings in a fascinating book, *The Serpent and the Rainbow*.

As for the resuscitating, mind-controlling drug, this was datura, obtained from the aptly named zombie cucumber *Datura stramonium*. Already known in other contexts to Western pharmacological researchers and also referred to as the thorn apple or jimson weed, its effects include delusions, mental confusion, disorientation, amnesia, and (if taken in sufficient doses) an impenetrable stupor – all typical zombie characteristics. Yet there was clearly more involved here than just this drug, because even when it was no longer administered the zombies rarely regained their normal mental state, remaining perpetually in a twilight world of semi-consciousness until the advent of true death.

In relation to this, Davis noted that if the paralysed, buried victims awaiting zombification are left in their coffins for any considerable period before being exhumed, they will experience oxygen starvation, resulting in irreversible brain damage that enhances datura's mind-numbing activities. The reason why Clairvius Narcisse became relatively lucid once his doses of datura ceased must, therefore, be because he had not been left in his coffin long enough to suffer

any significant degree of oxygen starvation before being dug up by the bokor.

An interesting side-discovery was made by Davis during his zombie revelations. Far from being innocent victims of evil bokors, it seems that those transformed into zombies were often people who had caused trouble themselves and, as a result of this, an angry relative or a jealous neighbour had sought revenge by hiring a bokor to turn them into zombies as a punishment.

From Davis's remarkable findings, it is clear that the traditional nightmarish concept of zombies as rotting corpses magically resurrected to life is nothing more than superstition, made real only by horror movies and pulp novels. Nevertheless, in one sense zombies can still be equated very accurately with the living dead. After all, to be drugged into immobility, pronounced dead and then buried alive in a coffin, exhumed by sorcerers and maintained ever afterwards in a constant state of brainwashed, brutalized servitude – if that isn't a fate worse than death itself, a veritable living death, then what is?

✹

# BLUE MEN OF THE MOUNTAINS

Almost 6000 metres (20,000 feet) above sea level, high in the Andean mountains of Chile, lives a community of miners whose members can be instantly distinguished from miners elsewhere in the world, and for a very good reason: their skin is bright blue!

These extraordinary people were brought to scientific attention by physiologist Dr John West from the University of California's School of Medicine at San Diego, who discovered them during a mountaineering trip. At first, the secret of their blue-coloured skin was a complete mystery, but over a period of time Dr West's studies uncovered the answer.

The miners' blue hue stems from oxygen deficiency at the lofty altitude at which they live (some 750 metres, or 2500 feet, higher than the previous

*The high Andes of Chile are home to a mining community living some 750 metres (2500 feet) higher than the previous record altitude for long-term human survival.*

record for long-term human survival), coupled with their active life-style. These two factors collectively induce the miners to produce greater than normal amounts of the oxygen-transporting blood pigment haemoglobin. This is bright red when oxygenated, carrying oxygen from the lungs to the body organs via the arteries; but it is blue when deoxygenated, travelling from the body organs back to the lungs via the veins.

Deoxygenated haemoglobin imparts a blue colouration to skin when present in the high concentration exhibited by these miners, because its colour is more readily visible through the skin than is the red shade of oxygenated haemoglobin.

Blue-skinned people are not unique to Chile. In Perry County, Kentucky, USA, there is a community characterized by (and nowadays very famous for) their pale-blue skin. Their history began in c.1800, when a boy with blue-tinted skin was born in France but later migrated to the USA, becoming resident on the relatively inaccessible, little-frequented

banks of Perry County's Troublesome Creek in the Ozark Mountains. Here he married a local woman and raised a family, whose members exhibited their father's curious trait.

This suggested that whereas the Chilean miners' blue skin is a product of direct physiological adaptation to unusual environmental conditions, in the case of the Troublesome Creek family an inherited mutant gene was responsible. And sure enough, as a result of longstanding inbreeding among the small, isolated community living here, the blue-skin trait persisted, producing a localized population of blue-skinned people.

During the 1960s, this fascinating case attracted the attention of Kentucky University haematologist Dr Madison Cawein. His studies revealed that the biochemical fault caused by the mutant gene, and resulting in the Troublesome Creek denizens' blue skin, was an inability to synthesize the enzyme that breaks down metahaemoglobin – a respiratory blood pigment that is distinctly blue-brown in colour. As it

happens, however, this condition can be simply but successfully treated by the regular administration of methylene blue, a common antiseptic that reverses the mutant gene's effect, thus transforming blue skin into normal pink skin.

# CHUPACABRAS

Since the 1970s, the Caribbean island of Puerto Rico has witnessed some decidedly bizarre events featuring a mystifying entity called the chupacabras ("goatsucker").

"Goatsucker" is also an alternative name for a group of inoffensive nocturnal birds more commonly known as nightjars, but judging from the Puerto Rican accounts, the chupacabras is not a bird and is anything but inoffensive! So far, it has been blamed for the savage deaths of many dogs, cats and livestock animals, even creatures as large as cattle and horses, whose grossly mutilated

*Grisly gourmet: the chupacabras or "goatsucker" is a grotesque predator with a penchant for blood and mutilation. Has it escaped from a genetic engineering laboratory, as some people believe?*

corpses have later been found drained of blood and minus various body organs that have been ripped out. In what must surely be the most grotesque incident from this particular category of chupacabras reports, however, the "victim" was a stuffed teddy bear, which the creature had reputedly destroyed at a house in Caguas before leaving behind a slimy puddle and a piece of rancid white meat on the windowsill!

The chupacabras's attacks upon animals are sinister enough, but its encounters with humans are infinitely stranger, as Scott Corrales has revealed in his invaluable 71-page report, *The Chupacabras Diaries*. At 6 a.m. on 26 March 1995, Jaime Torres was walking through a field containing a flock of sheep owned by farmer Enrique Barreto of Orocovis when he allegedly saw a chupacabras lying along a branch on a nearby tree, looking down at him. According to Torres, it had a round head, dark grey face, elongated black eyes, delicate jaw and small mouth. Even more distinctive, however, was its pigmentation: just like a surrealistic

chameleon it changed colour even as Torres stared at it, fluctuating from purple to brown to yellow. Yet its most bizarre talent was still to be revealed.

Suddenly, as Torres continued to look up at it, the chupacabras's head began to rock from side to side and the creature emitted an eerie hissing sound; as it did so, Torres became very dizzy, almost fainting. Losing no time, the creature dropped down from the tree and rapidly disappeared through the undergrowth, leaving its queasy observer far behind.

This same locality had previously been the site of a very similar encounter. In that case a police officer had been investigating a dead sheep on Barreto's estate when he spied a bipedal creature, 1 metre or so (3–4 feet) tall, with bright orange-yellow eyes peering at him from a shadowy area nearby. When the officer attempted to pursue this apparent chupacabras, however, he was instantly overcome by such an acute yet wholly unheralded attack of nausea and headache that he was forced to

abandon the chase and needed to be assisted by his partner back to their patrol car.

In another incident, the investigator Jorge Martín learnt that a Mrs Quiñones of Naranjito had recently seen a chupacabras the height of a three-year-old child, standing by some hedges. True to form, its gaze caused her to feel so nauseous that she was unable to follow when it fled away.

Based upon a considerable corpus of eyewitness descriptions, the chupacabras seemingly stands about 1–1.5 metres (3–5 feet) tall, with large slanted eyes (sometimes said to glow orange or red), bare holes instead of lobed ears, tiny holes in place of true nostrils and a small lipless mouth. It has long, thin arms with three clawed fingers on each hand and muscular long legs with three clawed toes on each foot. The grotesque animal's furry body is grey mottled with darker blotches, and glowing spines run from the crown of its head down the entire length of its back and continuously change colour.

No creature known to science bears the slightest resemblance to this entity, which has encouraged eyewitnesses and others to propose a number of more imaginative identities; these range from a UFO-originating alien to a grotesque, top-secret product of genetic engineering that has somehow absconded from its laboratory confines. Scientists have attempted to explain away the chupacabras's livestock kills as the work of escapee monkeys that are indeed known to exist here, but monkeys do not suck blood, they do not change colour and they certainly cannot render people physically ill simply by gazing at them. Little wonder that Scott Corrales has named this entity the paranormal predator of Puerto Rico.

As a tantalizing tail-piece, the two issues of *Strange Magazine* for 1995 contained reports by Corrales on the alleged corpse of a small but quite extraordinary entity that had been killed in Puerto Rico during the 1980s by a cattle rancher. Apparently, the rancher's farm had suffered many incidents of grisly animal livestock mutilations, so he had been mounting a vigil with two friends on the night in question when, to their amazement, four of these beings had entered his stables and had begun levitating one of his heifers! The slain creature's three companions escaped.

The reports' accompanying photo, one of 22 obtained by Jorge Martín from a Mr Rafael Baerga, depicts a creature strongly reminiscent of a chupacabras, sharing its round head, large slanting eyes, small lipless mouth, tiny nostrils, apparent lack of ears, and thin arms. However, the corpse's clawed hands each have *four* fingers, not three. Biologists to whom Martín showed the photos were unable to identify the creature, citing many noteworthy morphological idiosyncrasies when ruling out monkeys or a human foetus as realistic possibilities. At present, the unnamed cattle rancher who shot it is refusing to submit its corpse for formal analysis in case it is confiscated, so its identity remains unresolved.

❁

# THE BERMUDA TRIANGLE

The Bermuda Triangle has received intensive coverage and attention from the media world. Whether it actually exists in the real world, however, is another matter entirely.

According to a plethora of speculative reports, articles and books that appeared on this subject during the late 1960s and 1970s, the Bermuda Triangle is a mysterious expanse of sea in the western Atlantic where a disproportionately high number of ships and aircraft have supposedly vanished without trace over the years; this includes more than a hundred since 1945. The outermost geographical limits claimed for its baleful effects can be mapped to yield a triangle that links up the tip of Florida, Puerto Rico and Bermuda, thereby earning it its name, which was coined in 1964 by Vincent Gaddis, a veteran American investigator of mysteries.

Countless theories proposing how and why the Triangle exerts such deadly power have been aired. These range from attacks by sea monsters, abductions by extraterrestrials or subaquatic Atlanteans, and freak killer waves of gargantuan proportions, to sudden releases of methane bubbles from frozen lattices of ice on the sea-bed, a black hole beneath the waves, geomagnetic anomalies, and a giant submerged crystal warping the space around its victims (as suggested by Charles Berlitz in his bestseller *The Bermuda Triangle*).

One of the most frequently reiterated cases in the Bermuda Triangle file featured five US Navy Avenger torpedo-bomber planes called Flight 19. The squadron vanished while flying over this area of sea in bad weather on the evening of 5 December 1945, after setting off in good flying conditions that afternoon on a routine training mission from the Fort Lauderdale Naval Air Station. A Martin Mariner search plane sent to look for them also went missing.

Many accounts of this incident claim that in a series of strange messages transmitted by the bombers' leader, Lieutenant Charles C. Taylor, before

*The **Marine Sulphur Queen**, which disappeared in 1963, is one of many vessels which have supposedly been lost without trace inside the Bermuda Triangle.*

their disappearance, he stated: "We seem to be off course ... everything is wrong ... strange ... even the ocean doesn't look as it should ... it looks like we are...." No further words were received. Yet when this was investigated by Lawrence D. Kusche, a research librarian at Arizona State University and author of the much-acclaimed book *The Bermuda Triangle – Solved*, he found that there was no evidence whatsoever to suggest that Taylor had ever spoken those words.

An official Navy report concluded that both of Taylor's compasses had failed and he had mistaken his squadron's position, led astray by the similarity in appearance between the Bahamas and the Florida Keys (the islands that they should have been flying over). In trying to relocate their correct position, he and his squadron would have run out of fuel, crashing into the sea that night. The darkness would have hidden any debris from search parties. At 7.50 p.m., the SS *Gaines Mills* sighted a plane catching fire above the sea near Daytona Beach before hitting the water and exploding. This is believed to have been the lost search plane.

Kusche and other serious researchers have also exposed significant discrepancies between popular reports of many additional Bermuda Triangle cases and the verifiable facts concerning them. Indeed, as David Group emphasizes in *The Evidence for the Bermuda Triangle*, it is very apparent that the supposed "evidence" is principally founded upon factual errors, misinterpretations and overt distortions of the facts behind the cited cases. Almost all of these cases, in fact, can be readily shown to have a perfectly natural rather than an unnatural explanation.

Perhaps the most telling blow to the much-hyped Bermuda Triangle was struck by the shipping insurers, Lloyd's of London, in a letter of 4 April 1975 to the magazine *Fate*: "According to Lloyd's Records, 428 vessels have been reported missing throughout the world since 1955, and it may interest you to know that our intelligence service can find no evidence to support the claim that the 'Bermuda Triangle' has more losses than elsewhere."

# THE MOVING COFFINS OF BARBADOS

One of the most famous unsolved Caribbean mysteries features the unnervingly mobile coffins formerly housed in the Chase family's vault at Christ Church, in the south-west of Barbados. The vault was purchased in 1807 by Thomas Chase, a plantation owner, and by 1812 three members of his family had died. The first two had been entombed inside its walls without incident, but when the vault was opened again to admit the coffin of the third, attendants were shocked to discover that the two coffins already present had apparently been disturbed, for their positions had changed. From then on, with the sole exception of Thomas Chase's own burial on 9 August 1812, each time that a member of the Chase family died and the vault was reopened, similar scenes of disarray met the eyes of the ever-increasing throng of morbid onlookers eager to view this macabre sight for themselves.

Yet there were no footprints in the sand covering the vault's floor, and even secret seals deliberately hidden by investigators were found not to have been tampered with when next the vault was opened. Only the positions of the coffins changed, nothing else.

In 1820, the mystery was brought to an unresolved end when Viscount Combermere, Governor of Barbados, ordered all the coffins to be removed and reburied in fresh graves nearby. Many explanations have been offered for their unwonted restlessness, including seismic tremors, poltergeist activity, flooding and even an elaborate Masonic hoax, but none has been verified. All that we do know is that the Chase family's "haunted vault" has remained empty ever afterwards, and its coffins have shown no desire to wander since their reburial.

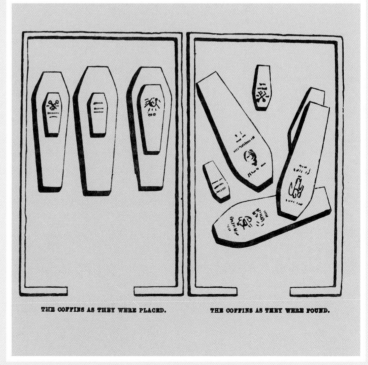

THE COFFINS AS THEY WERE PLACED.    THE COFFINS AS THEY WERE FOUND.

*A contemporary plan shows the disarray of coffins in the Chase family vault after their last disturbance, in 1820.*

# The Ancient Ways

## AYERS ROCK – THE MYSTICAL ALLURE OF ULURU

To Westerners and Western science, it is Ayers Rock – the world's largest natural monolith. Situated about 320 kilometres (200 miles) south-east of Alice Springs in the Northern Territory of Australia, this enormous block of arkose sandstone stands 348 metres (1142 feet) high and is up to 3 kilometres (2 miles) long. In addition, it may extend 6 kilometres (3¾ miles) down beneath the earth's surface, thus concealing the greater part of its true bulk in a fashion akin to a terrestrial iceberg.

To the aboriginal peoples of Australia, however, it is called Uluru and constitutes the most sacred site on this vast island continent. It is a place of pilgrimage across the arid desert for aboriginals from every region of Australia. Technically, Uluru is owned by two local tribes, the Yankunitjatjara and the Pitjantjatjara, and many of the caves around its perimeter, which measures over 8 kilometres (5 miles), contain sacred paintings depicting the Dreamtime.

The Dreamtime is the aboriginal concept of Creation – when the world and all that it contains came into being. It was a time very different from today, peopled by gods and heroes whose bodies and songs gave rise to the mountains, the lakes and the stars, and by ancient spirit beings and magical beasts (see p. 40) that populated the lands with Australia's unique fauna and

*Ayers Rock: to Australia's aboriginal peoples the most sacred place on earth.*

flora. And every crack, every pebble, every rocky outgrowth on Uluru is invested with a specific Dreamtime story or meaning for its aboriginal guardians.

In recent times, however, this belief has come into conflict with a modern Western threat – tourism. Uluru is famed for its spectrum of highly photogenic colour changes each

morning as the rising sun bestows ever more sunlight upon its craggy surface, transforming its sable evening tones into deep mauve and thence into a shimmering pink hue. This magnificent sight has drawn White Australians and tourists from overseas to visit Ayers Rock in their millions every year, but not all are satisfied merely to see its awesome majesty. All too often, tourists decide to take back home a souvenir of Uluru – sometimes a pebble, sometimes a sizeable lump of rock.

Needless to say, in the eyes of the aboriginal peoples such acts are a desecration and have caused great consternation, but Uluru appears to be solving the problem in its own mystical but highly effective manner. In February 1996, Julian Barry, senior ranger at Ayers Rock, revealed that numerous tourists are returning their pilfered souvenirs (sometimes personally, more often by post), convinced that they are cursed and have brought them bad luck.

One Londoner claimed that shortly after taking a piece of rock from Uluru, he was struck down by gout; an American cited the sudden ill-health of his mother after bringing home a rocky souvenir from Uluru; many others have suffered bankruptcy. Are these mere coincidences, or is the magic of the Dreamtime still as potent today as it was in the beginning?

# ANCESTRAL BEINGS AND SPIRIT BEASTS

According to the Dreamtime (Creation) myths of Australia's aboriginal tribes, in the early days of the world there were many strange types of ancestral spirit entities. These magical beasts and beings are dismissed by modern science as fantasy, but the aboriginals firmly believe that they still exist today – if you know where to look for them.

The Wiradjuri aboriginals who live in the central west of New South Wales say that some of this region's lonely stretches of countryside and even its rivers are frequented by hairy dog-like animals known as the mirrii or mirriuula. These magic animals are often quite small when first seen, but the longer you stare at them, the larger they grow! They can often grow to the size of a calf or even a pony in just a few moments, and then, without warning, they will disappear. Some mirrii dogs are dangerous, because when they see someone they will follow him and try to lure him into the depths of their river.

The Wiradjuri also speak of the yuurii, which are hairy little men and women, no more than a metre (3 feet) tall, but with long fingernails and big teeth. The yuurii men have long beards too. The Gumbangirr aboriginals, who also live in New South Wales, call these tiny people the bitarr and say that they particularly enjoy playing with aboriginal children.

The aboriginals of Victoria are familiar with some other types of mysterious pygmy. The nyols are small, stony-grey humanoid beings who allegedly inhabit caverns in the deep rocks beneath the surface of the land, but occasionally they come up above ground to frolic and play amid the shadows of dusk. In contrast, the net-nets have brown skin, long sharp claws instead of fingernails and live among the rocks above ground. Stranger still is the pot-koorok, a small man-frog with great webbed feet, long mobile fingers and a wet pear-shaped body. It dwells in rivers and deep pools. Arnhem Land's rock crevasses may still be home to stick-like spirits known as the mimi, similar in form to Queensland's quinkins – embodiments of lust.

And then there is Old Red-Eye. This is the name given to an often insubstantial entity, or one of only vaguely human form, that can materialize anywhere, at any time, and

*This aboriginal rock painting in northern Queensland depicts the stick-like quinkin spirits.*

Island has attracted great scientific interest, owing to its enigmatic giant statues (moai), numbering around a thousand. Who made them, and why?

Researchers now believe that Easter Island was first settled in c.AD 400, and for several centuries afterwards the islanders created skilfully carved, sun-oriented terraces and small statues. These resembled various pre-Columbian Andean examples (i.e. dating from the period before Columbus's discovery of the New World). By AD 1100, however, they were converting the terraces into ceremonial platforms (ahu), and were creating the first stone giants, carved directly from the crater walls of Rano Raraku, a dormant volcano.

These statues were slid down the hillside into a standing position, where they were completed and polished before being taken to the ahu and placed on top of them, facing inland. Their function remains controversial, but according to modern-day islanders they were monuments to dead rulers and were once infused with benevolent supernatural power (mana). Intriguingly, various geomagnetic anomalies have been recorded from Easter Island, so could it be possible that these monoliths acted as foci for healing earth energy, as proposed for standing stones in Britain and elsewhere in the world?

At first, the statues varied in form from one another, but later examples all depicted the same man (whose identity is unknown). Each was carved only as far down as the top of his legs, and portrayed him with a heavy brow, lantern jaws, jutting chin, aquiline nose, very long ear-lobes and a red topknot (pukao) on his head. The topknots were carved from a small volcanic cone called Puna Pau. Most statues weighed 25–40 tonnes and stood 3.5–7.5 metres (12–25 feet) tall, but over the years they were carved ever larger by the islanders: one incomplete example still lying inside the crater at Rano Raraku weighs about 270 tonnes and is around 21 metres (70 feet) long.

This is only one of about 400 unfinished statues found in the crater. The reason why these were never completed was a violent civil war on the island, between the Hanau Eepe or Long-Ears, who were apparently the ruling class, and the Hanau Momoko or

which can mesmerize a person with a fixed glare from its bright red eyes. Time stands still for the victims of Old Red-Eye, held in thrall for however long it chooses to gaze at them, and even if they should succeed in calling out for help, no one is ever able to hear them.

Even more sinister is the yara-ma-yha-who. According to aboriginal folklore, this is a tiny toothless frog-like man that lives in fig trees and has suckers on its hands. If any children should see it, they must run away at once, because the yara-ma-yha-who is a merciless vampire, who will immediately jump down on top of them from out of the tree, clasp them with its suckers and drain them of their blood!

Mirrii dogs, net-nets, pot-kooroks, yara-ma-yha-whos and the other magical dream beasts are rarely reported nowadays, for their time was long ago – but time is never still, and one day theirs may come again.

✷

# EASTER ISLAND, LAND OF THE LONG-EARS

Lying roughly 4350 kilometres (2700 miles) east of Tahiti, 4200 (2600) west of Valparaiso in Chile and 3200 (2000) south-west of the Galapagos Islands in the south Pacific, Easter Island is the world's loneliest inhabited locality, as Thor Heyerdahl observed in *Aku-Aku*, recording his 1955–56 expedition here.

The island first became known to the Western world when it was discovered by the Dutch sea voyager Admiral Jacob Roggeveen on 5 April 1722; this was Easter Sunday, hence the island's Western name. Ever since then, Easter

*Early Easter Island statues vary in form, but later examples – such as this, near the Rano Raraku crater – portray the same unknown man.*

*Wooden tablets and a lost language: could these solve the riddle of how civilization sprang up in one of the world's most remote places?*

remains undeciphered. In 1888, Chile claimed Easter Island and since then the population of native islanders has gradually increased, so that they now number more than 2000. Around 30 of the giant statues have been erected again too, by visiting scientific teams.

But where did the very first inhabitants of Easter Island come from? According to traditional schools of thought, they originated solely from the Polynesian islands to the west, whose inhabitants in turn came from Asia. Thor Heyerdahl, however, was not convinced that this was the entire story, and during his researches on Easter Island in the mid-1950s he obtained some intriguing evidence to support his conviction that migration to this far-flung outpost may also have occurred from the east, by pre-Inca people from Peru.

The evidence on Easter Island that Heyerdahl has cited in favour of his hypothesis includes: the presence here of a freshwater plant called the totora reed native to Lake Titicaca in the Andes, and also the Andean sweet potato; early Easter Island drawings of reed boats and statues that recall versions found in the ancient city of Tiahuanaco near Bolivia's border with Peru; the former presence of sun worship here and in early Peruvian cultures; the existence here and in Andean cultures of fair-skinned red-haired people; plus the occurrence of the stone giants' long ear-lobe characteristic in Andean legends about the Tiahuanacan deity Con-Tici Viracocha. Demonstrating that such a migration would have been possible in those far-off days, Heyerdahl had previously built an early-Peruvian-style balsawood raft (named the Kon-Tiki) and sailed across the Pacific from Peru to the Tuamotu Archipelago in his famous voyage of 1947.

Geographer Robert Langdon has also offered support for this notion by disclosing in 1988 that tapioca, derived from South America's manioc plant, had been found to be part of the Easter Island people's diet as long ago as 1770, by an expedition led by Captain Felipe Gonzalez. Unfortunately, this notable fact subsequently became obscured owing to a mistranslation of manioc's local name in 1908 by historian Bolton

Short-Ears, who were their underlings. In 1680, the war culminated in a battle on the Poike peninsula, in which the Short-Ears triumphed, killing all but one of the Long-Ears, and 42 years later the island's long period of isolation from European contact came to an end with its discovery by Roggeveen. In 1774, Captain Cook arrived, and found that some time in the previous 50 years the stone giants had been knocked off their platforms during fresh outbreaks of war and were lying haphazardly on the ground – but far worse was to follow in 1862.

This was when a Peruvian slave ship abducted most of Easter Island's men, transporting them back to Peru to work in the mines. The majority died, and of the few that survived and were returned to their island home following the intervention of Tahiti's bishop, all were infected with smallpox. Inevitably, this virulent disease decimated Easter Island's already much-depleted population: by 1877 it totalled a mere 111 people. One of the many consequences of this terrible saga of suffering was the death of every islander who could read their unique picture writing (called rongo-rongo and carved on wooden slabs). Even today, it

Corney within his definitive account of the expedition – an error that remained uncorrected until Langdon's revelation 80 years later.

Even so, the notion of ancient South American settlement here is still not fully accepted in scientific circles, so the mystery surrounding the origins of Easter Island's civilization remains unresolved. Ironically, the answer to this riddle may already exist, locked away in the various surviving samples of Easter Island's cryptic rongo-rongo language, but until (if ever) the key to its linguistic secret is uncovered, we shall never know for sure.

# FIRE-WALKING

Originally a rite of spring, and performed in many parts of the world, including India, Greece, South Africa and California, fire-walking is most popularly associated with Polynesia, especially the Society Islands and the Fijian Islands. In 1901, engineering scientist Professor S.P. Langley from the Smithsonian Institution witnessed a classic demonstration of fire-walking in Tahiti, performed by a native priest from the

neighbouring Society island of Raiatea. The demonstration featured a trench measuring 6.4 metres (21 feet) long, 2.75 metres (9 feet) across and about 0.6 metre (2 feet) deep, filled with radiant basalt rocks piled on top of blazing logs. The priest and several of his acolytes strode steadily but very briskly over this trench four times, with no resulting injury. Yet when Langley levered one of the rocks out of it and into a bucket of water, the water churned and frothed so violently that a considerable quantity boiled over the sides.

In 1950, Dr Harry B. Wright of Philadelphia observed a similar fire-

*Many fire-walkers expose the soles of their feet to temperatures as high as 800°C.*

walking ceremony, performed annually by the people of Mbengga, one of the smaller Fijian islands. Before the fire-walk began, Wright examined the feet of the participants, to determine whether they had been treated with any protective substance, but he found no evidence to suggest this. Paradoxically, he did discover that although these people experienced no injury or pain whatsoever when walking across their trench of fiery rocks, their feet displayed normal sensitivity to the approach of a lighted cigarette and also to a pinprick.

Many other fire-walking demonstrations have been closely monitored by scientists, who confirm that the walkers' feet have not been treated in any way, that the temperature of the rocks has been shown to be as high as 800°C, and that even untrained Westerners can successfully perform fire-walking – as long as they firmly believe that they will not be harmed by the fire. How can this astonishing accomplishment be explained?

The answer seems to be a subtle blend of several different interacting factors. The soles of the feet of native fire-walkers are very thick and calloused, which would reduce injury. Moreover, during an investigation in

1935, the English psychical researcher Harry Price noted that physical contact between the *entirety* of each of the walker's feet and the fiery rocks lasts no more than half a second at a time (hence actual contact by any *specific* part of that foot is even less). Thus there is insufficient time for the feet to be burnt, especially if the total length of the walk is itself brief. Tellingly, after watching some local people undertake a three-second fire-walk at the 26th annual meeting of the Ceylon Association for the Advancement of Science, Dr Carlo Fonseka challenged them to perform a 30-second fire-walk: they all declined to do so.

As Professor Jearl Walker, a physicist at Cleveland State University in Ohio, has pointed out, a phenomenon very relevant to fire-walking is the Leidenfrost effect. This is the process whereby a liquid exposed to intense heat will instantly form a protective, insulating boundary layer composed of steam. It allows us all to indulge in a very simple form of fire-walking – when we snuff out a candle with a wet finger. And sure enough, many observers at fire-walking ceremonies have noted that the walkers often moisten their feet before performing the walk.

Psychology is also most important. Westerners performing fire-walking after convincing themselves that the glowing rocks will not harm them not only escape injury but also experience feelings of euphoria. This suggests an enhanced secretion by the brain of endorphins – natural pain-killers that impart an elevated sense of happiness and well-being. Just another demonstration that the power of the mind is indeed a potent force.

✦

## BOOYA STONES

In Steven Spielberg's classic adventure film *Indiana Jones and the Temple of Doom*, starring Harrison Ford, the eponymous hero embarks upon a quest to regain some stolen sacred stones that are able to radiate an eerie glowing light. All this, of course, is fiction – whereas the booya stones from the Murray Islands are an extraordinary fact.

The Murray Islands are situated in the Torres Strait, separating the Cape York peninsula in Queensland from Papua New Guinea. The booya stones (of which at least three were known)

*Stones that radiate an eerie glowing light: more than just enjoyable film fantasy?*

were formerly retained by the Murray Islands' priesthood, who had apparently passed them down from generation to generation since time immemorial.

These remarkable objects have been researched in detail by Australian travel writer Ion Idriess, who revealed that they emitted a blue light of such intensity that when it was concentrated into a beam by a special holding device and pointed at a human, an X-ray effect was observed and it was invariably followed by that person's death. Idriess speculated that they may have been lumps of pure radium, but their identity has never been conclusively ascertained, for with the onset of European control in Australasia, the Murray Islands' priests hid their revered stones in secret caves. Perhaps a real-life Indiana Jones is needed, to rediscover not only their hideaway but also the key to their formidably potent power.

✦

# WHISTLING GHOSTS AND DEATH CLICKS

During the first half of this century, Sir Arthur Grimble was an administrator in the Gilbert and Ellice Islands (now the independent Pacific republics of Kiribati and Tuvalu respectively), and it was here that he encountered the whistling ghosts of Arorae, a tiny coral isle in the Southern Gilbert group.

Towards the end of a long sea voyage to Arorae, Grimble was told by fellow passengers that his friend Tabanea, the sorcerer of Tarawa, had died two evenings before from a sudden stroke. Yet Tabanea had been in good health when Grimble had last seen him a week earlier, and there had been no ship in the area recently to bring news from Tarawa anyway. Consequently, Grimble dismissed the story as unfounded gossip; but when he arrived at Arorae, he received precisely the same account from a wholly independent source. Once again, however, Arorae had not been visited recently by anyone, so where had such a rumour originated?

*In the Gilbert Islands, ancient understandings put the paranormal into context.*

Making enquiries, Grimble learnt that on Arorae it had come from an extremely old wise-woman called Nei Watia, who had in turn received it from a mysterious but entirely infallible source – the taani-kanimomoi, or whistlers. These are supposedly the ghosts of recently dead relations, who inhabit the air and fly up and down the islands, seeing and hearing everything that happens and passing news of their findings to people who can understand their whistling speech.

Wishing to learn more about these remarkable entities, Grimble visited Nei Watia, and once he was inside her thatched shack she called out to the whistlers. Immediately, the entire shack was filled with a shrill multitudinous whistling, like a host of invisible crickets or strident disembodied

birdsong. It occurred at the same time as Nei Watia was speaking, thereby ruling out ventriloquism.

Perplexed but still not convinced, Grimble eventually departed Arorae, aboard a boat homeward-bound for Tarawa. As soon as he docked at Tarawa, however, he was met by a throng of people who informed him that his friend Tabanea had unexpectedly died – from a stroke and at the exact time reported (via Nei Wadia) by the whistling ghosts of Arorae.

A comparably bizarre phenomenon has also been documented from Samoa. Instead of whistling ghosts that spread news, however, it features the sudden onset of loud and persistent clicking sounds throughout the house of someone who is about to die.

# INDEX

## Picture Credits

The publishers would like to thank the following sources for their kind permission to reproduce the pictures in this book:

British Film Institute Slide Collection; Bruce Coleman Ltd.; Corbis; Enigmas Magazine, Spain; Mary Evans Picture Library/Zora Hurston; Fortean Picture Library; Maureen Gavin Picture Library; Images Colour Library/Horizon; Frank Lane Picture Agency; Museum of Mankind; Rex Features Ltd.; Dr. K P N Shuker; South American Pictures/Tony Morrison; Strange Magazine, USA

Every effort has been made to acknowledge correctly and contact the source and/or copyright holder of each picture, and Carlton Books Limited apologizes for any unintentional errors or omissions which will be corrected in future editions of this book.

# About the Author

Dr Karl P.N. Shuker is a zoologist, lecturer and writer who specializes in cryptozoology and animal mythology. A scientist with a longstanding interest in unexplained phenomena of all kinds, Dr Shuker has amassed a considerable archive of material during many years of personal research. He is a regular contributor to *Strange*, America's most credible magazine dedicated to exploring unexplained phenomena. Dr Shuker's books include *The Lost Ark: New and Rediscovered Animals of the 20th Century*, and *Mystery Cats of the World*. He acted as consultant to Reader's Digest on *Almanac of the Uncanny*; *Secrets of the Natural World*; *Man and Beast* and to Guinness on the *Guinness Book of Records*.